THE HAPPY HUNTING-GROUNDS

Arab sheikhs who had ridden in, camel-back, from the desert
to pay their respects

THE HAPPY HUNTING-GROUNDS

Kermit Roosevelt
Author of *War in the Garden of Eden*

Illustrated from Photographs by the Author

Introduction by Jennifer Ham

BARNES & NOBLE BOOKS

NEW YORK

To
The Mistress of Sagamore

CONTENTS

LIST OF ILLUSTRATIONS IX

INTRODUCTION XI

I. THE HAPPY HUNTING-GROUNDS 1

II. IN QUEST OF SABLE ANTELOPE 27

III. THE SHEEP OF THE DESERT 36

IV. AFTER MOOSE IN NEW BRUNSWICK 52

V. TWO BOOK-HUNTERS IN SOUTH AMERICA 64

VI. SETH BULLOCK—SHERIFF OF THE BLACK
HILLS COUNTRY 79

ENDNOTES 99

SUGGESTED READING 101

LIST OF ILLUSTRATIONS

ARAB SHEIKHS WHO HAD RIDDEN IN, CAMEL-BACK,
FROM THE DESERT TO PAY THEIR RESPECTS   *Frontispiece*

SIR ALFRED PEASE'S SKETCH OF OUR
FIRST GIRAFFE HUNT   *following*   12

FATHER AND R. H. MUNRO FERGUSON AT THE
ELKHORN RANCH, AFTER THE RETURN FROM
A SUCCESSFUL HUNTING TRIP   *following*   18

FACSIMILE OF A PICTURE LETTER BY FATHER   *following*   20

PUTTING THE TAPE ON A TUSKER   *following*   22

LAUNCHING A NEWLY MADE DUGOUT ON THE DÚVIDA   *following*   24

A RELIC OF THE PORTUGUESE OCCUPATION;
AN OLD WELL BESIDE THE TRAIL   *following*   28

THE DEATH DANCE OF THE WA NYIKA CHILDREN
IN MEMORY OF THE CHIEFTAIN'S LITTLE SON   *following*   30

ACROSS THE BAY FROM MOMBASA; THE PORTERS
READY TO SHOULDER LOADS AND MARCH   *following*   34

LIST OF ILLUSTRATIONS

A DESERT CAMP IN OLD MEXICO   *following* 40

CASARES ON HIS WHITE MULE   *following* 44

MAKING FAST THE SHEEP'S HEAD   *following* 48

A NOONDAY HALT ON THE WAY DOWN RIVER,
RETURNING FROM THE HUNTING COUNTRY   *following* 54

BRINGING OUT THE TROPHIES OF THE HUNT   *following* 58

THE CAPTAIN MAKES ADVANCES TO
A LITTLE INDIAN GIRL   *following* 80

A MORNING'S BAG OF PRAIRIE CHICKEN
IN SOUTH DAKOTA   *following* 90

INTRODUCTION

> "I am fond of politics, but fonder still
> of a little big-game hunting."
> — Theodore Roosevelt

IN April 1909 young Kermit Roosevelt left his studies at Harvard University and set out with his father, Theodore Roosevelt, the twenty-sixth president of the United States, on a year-long adventure into the wilds of eastern Africa. His father, now fifty and blinded in his left eye by a boxing injury, was relying both on Kermit's youth to compensate for his own lost physical ability and on his ability to write and work with the camera to ensure that the right image of their regal adventure made it to press. Preparations for what was to be the largest and most ambitious hunting expedition ever in Kenya began in his childhood home, the White House, a year before, where a practice firing range was set up to assist in honing their marksmanship skills. They enlisted the advice of the well-traveled Frederick Selous and Edward North Buxton and the expertise of Kenya's two most famous hunters, R. J. Cuninghame and William Judd, and engaged Nairobi's premier safari outfitter. The expedition departed amidst great fanfare aboard the German steamship *Hamburg* from New York harbor and met up with the *Admiral* from Naples for the journey across the Red Sea and Indian Ocean to Mombasa. While an already impressive undertaking, this was only the beginning of the

Roosevelts' travels. Five years later the father-son team set out again to explore the Amazon jungles of Brazil and fifteen years later Kermit embarked on another hunting trip to China with his brother in search of great pandas. Theirs was a time of exploration, a time immortalized by his personal friend, Rudyard Kipling, whose far-flung tales of adventures excited the imaginations of the Roosevelt children in their childhood and inspired Kermit in particular to set out to explore some of the world's most remote territories as a kind of rough rider in his own rite. Like so many big-game hunters and explorers before him, Kermit turned to writing, recounting some of these almost incredible real-life adventures in this eloquent and unvarnished gem, *The Happy Hunting-Grounds*.

Kermit Roosevelt, was born in Oyster Bay, Long Island, New York in 1889, the second child of five children in the Roosevelt family. As his siblings had, he attended public school and later transferred to Groton, the prestigious Connecticut prep school, where his father had also been a student. Although gone from university for a year on safari, he still managed to complete an accelerated degree at Harvard, after which he worked as a manager in the National City Bank in Buenos Aires and took off again on expedition to the Amazon. At the beginning of WWI, he married the daughter of an American ambassador to Spain in Madrid and enlisted as a captain in the British armed forces in Mesopotamia. His military experiences fighting with the British can be found in his *War in the Garden of Eden* (1919). Having contracted malaria, he was then transferred to the United States army in France until the end of the war, after which he established and ran the lucrative Roosevelt Steamship Lines in the 1920s. It was then in his late twenties and thirties that he began documenting his wildlife adventures in *The Happy Hunting-Grounds* (1920). The volume opens with his account of the Mombasa hunting expedition in equatorial Africa followed by the tales of later treks taken after his return to his studies, his trips to the American Southwest to hunt mountain sheep, explorations into the Canadian and South Dakotan outback, the Mexican desert, and with his father, almost a decade after Conrad's *Heart of Darkness* (1902), into the heart of the Amazon in the Brazilian wilderness to trace the uncharted River of Doubt (Rio Roosevelt), a harrowing trip which almost cost his father's life. The narratives, while providing readers with a privileged look into the private life of Teddy Roosevelt as both father and outdoorsman, are also fascinating historical accounts of the sport of big-game hunting and count among some of the first authentic and unapologetic reactions of "civilized" Westerners to wilderness and other cultures at the turn of the century. One can imagine from the wealth of priceless original photos and drawings by Kermit, who was also the photographer and press liaison on many of these expeditions, that his travel experiences must have seemed to him like childhood adventure stories come to life. After completing *East of the Sun, West of the Moon* (1926), his account of collecting fauna in Eastern Turkistan, and *Trailing the Great Panda* (1929), which appeared after searching for pandas with his brother in the hinterlands of Tibet, Kermit ran into hard times in the Depression, became an alcoholic, and resigned before being recomissioned under Churchill and serving the British army in Norway and Egypt. Kermit's wife arranged for him to be stationed in the desolate U.S. army post at Fort Richardson, Alaska, where he assisted in bombing raids against the Japanese in the Aleutian Islands in WWII. But his bouts of depression never left him, and he committed suicide in Alaska in 1943, where he is buried.

Kermit's early literary experiences, transmitted as they were through the powerful figure of his father, indeed had a lasting influence on his imagination and the direction his life would take. An accomplished writer of adventure tales himself, Teddy Roosevelt initiated all of his sons at an early age into a pedagogy of both sports and literature. He proudly acknowledges the result of Kermit's upbringing in a letter he wrote to Ethel on their African journey: "It is rare for a boy with his refined tastes and his genuine appreciation of literature—and of so much else—to be also an exceptionally bold and hardy sportsman." For him, adventure literature, whether written by their family friend Rudyard Kipling, Henry Thoreau, Jack London, or published in sportsmen's magazines, as the actual adventures themselves, was an opportunity for boys to learn about nature, but also about becoming men. Roosevelt rejected romantic depictions of blissful nature as he did Mark Twain's protests against hunting, insisting instead on nature's inherent violence and cruelty, which he felt justified man's vigorous uses of power. The late Victorian era was after all the age of Darwinism, which featured an aggressive confidence in the triumph of the fit. For the nineteenth-century American male, on display in public sports like boxing and big-game hunting, fitness implied both physical and moral superiority and was an essential ingredient of, indeed equated with "manliness," an idea of exceptional importance to contemporary males and in particular to the identity of Theodore Roosevelt and his "Rough Riders," (his well-known cavalry unit of a few hundred Dakota and other cowboys, Ivy league football players, New York City cops, and about fifteen Native Americans). Despite recent evolutionary theory and conservationist policy, for the Roosevelts nature was still man's proving ground and the sport of hunting created the space for that contest to be dramatized.

As a result, hunting narratives were tremendously popular at the time with the male reading public of all ages, especially with Kermit's father, who was an avid collector, particularly of those books dealing with the chase of exotic big game; such as John Barrow's *Account of Travels into the Interior of Southern Africa* (1804) and Samuel and William Daniell's *Sketches Representing the Native Tribes, Animals and Scenery of Southern Africa* (1820). Big-game hunting had from the start been identified with upper-class hegemony and it was initially within this class amongst the world's most privileged that such tales found their audience. Even by the end of the nineteenth century big game literature still remained "short and simple annals of the rich," despite some democratization of the sport encouraged in part by the evolution of the steam engine, which allowed less wealthy writers as well access to those remote site locations. The genre eventually became conventionalized, typically beginning with some reference to trip planning and the ceremony of cleaning guns. The stories proceeded to mention supply statistics, the astounding size of the hunting party (sometimes including as many as 9,000 individuals), and the exotic meats consumed during the ordeal. The numerous difficulties and dangers encountered along a trail are then emphasized to magnify the hunters' accomplishments, and finally there is the trophy count, synecdochic proof for the taxidermist of the vanquished. Told from a first-person narrative perspective, these tales, while recounting boisterous male camaraderie in wilderness encampments, also often revealed their blunders, misjudgment, setbacks, and overcome fears in order to heighten readers' appreciation for the difficulty of the challenges confronting them. These accounts took what might have been frivolous tales of self-serving wealthy vacationers and enlarged them into valiant inspirations of male braggadocio, courage, and prowess. It is not clear where Kermit first encountered this literary form, but, although he does not include information about their travels prior to their arrival in the African bush in his first narrative, we do know that he made the acquaintance of Frederick Selous, one of the great masters of the genre, who entertained the hunting party for days on board the *Admiral* from Naples to Mombasa with his hunting tales of Africa, while Kermit's father recounted his frontier stories. If the spoils of the big-game hunter powerfully evoked the conquest and domination of exotic territories, written accounts, such as Kermit's, made his exploits seem still more inspiring and more widely accessible. Even more than the trophy collections, the narratives written by the protagonists fanned public appreciation of the heroic big-game hunter, who, having engaged in Hemmingway-type contests of brute cunning between man and nature, emerged as both the ideal and the definitive type of the empire builder.

During the late Victorian era at the height of imperialism, it was fashionable for European political leaders intent on preserving their remote protectorates to assert their ownership not only by publicizing their presence in foreign lands by being photographed there, but also by adorning their residences back home with animal souvenirs collected in these lands. The hunting exploits of Roosevelt's contemporary political leaders, such as those of Germany's Wilhelm II and the Prince of Wales, were already legendary in Europe. Such extravagant expeditions, the likes of which have rarely been seen since, yielded not only notoriety and bragging rights to these male leaders, but also served to bring these northern societies into contact with formerly unknown exotic cultures and ecosystems. Some of the rare wildlife bagged on these ventures, the lions, hippopotami, giraffes, ostriches, and wapiti, was given away as diplomatic gifts to other leaders, either for their walls or for their small resident menageries. Other animals were sold to the entertainment sector, to public zoos and circuses. The remaining specimens became the property of science academies and museums of natural history, which typically financed the expeditions and used them to expand their collections. Kermit's expedition in chapter one to Africa, in chapter three to the Mexican desert, and his trek to collect moose, caribou, and beaver in Canada in chapter four, were all conducted under the auspices and support of the National Museum of Natural History, a branch of the Smithsonian Institute. The African safari was further underwritten by *Scribner's Magazine,* who promised Kermit's father an additional $50,000 for twelve articles on the journey. Similarly, his hunting expedition to China was supported by the Chicago Field Museum of Natural History and perhaps not surprisingly he was later made president of the Audubon Society, a trustee of the American Museum of Natural History, and vice president of the Bronx Zoological Society. Naturally, for the investment, these organizations expected to be rewarded with significant spoils for their animal and plant collections. From the one scandalous African safari alone, the

Roosevelts brought back 14,000 specimens, among them count-less elephants, rhinos, hippopotami, zebras, giraffes, buffalo, and lions. While clearly embarked on for scientific and political profit, the public accounts of national presidents on hunting holiday at the turn of the century typically emphasized the sheer sport of these frivolous expeditions.

While there is no doubt that these adventures had educa-tional value for zoologists and anthropologists, the real reward of these costly enterprises was the adornment of political image, a kind of triumph over the animal and tribal kingdoms, an aggressive vitality, and strength of leadership. The prospect of political gain was behind the Roosevelt adventures as well. Throughout his presidency, Kermit's father, like no other before him, worked tirelessly to put the nation's natural resources and wilderness protection on the American political agenda. Despite the influential power of lobbyists from bur-geoning industries, his campaign to introduce the country's first conservation legislation and add 150 million acres to the national forest and park system was successful and with the Reclamation Act of 1902, he reclaimed countless acres of eroded land and reestablished it as game reserves. His success rested in no small part on popularizing the notion of taming wilderness, in bringing remote wilds into the public's experi-ence, in part through wilderness-park vacations and through the literary discourse of wilderness writing. Ultimately, these American narratives of imperialist adventures into nature allowed average citizens to engage, at least by proxy, in a kind of reenactment of conquest that had previously been confined to the privileged classes. The connection between triumphing over a dangerous animal and subduing native cultures was direct and obvious, and the association of the big-game hunter with the march of empire was literal as well as metonymic.

Jennifer Ham is a writer and scholar who lives in Wisconsin.

CHAPTER I

THE HAPPY HUNTING-GROUNDS

THERE is a universal saying to the effect that it is when men are off in the wilds that they show themselves as they really are. As is the case with the majority of proverbs there is much truth in it, for without the minor comforts of life to smooth things down, and with even the elemental necessities more or less problematical, the inner man has an unusual opportunity of showing himself— and he is not always attractive. A man may be a pleasant companion when you always meet him clad in dry clothes, and certain of substantial meals at regulated intervals, but the same cheery individual may seem a very different person when you are both on half rations, eaten cold, and have been drenched for three days— sleeping from utter exhaustion, cramped and wet.

My father had done much hunting with many and varied friends. I have often heard him say of some one whom I had thought an ideal hunting companion: "He's a good fellow, but he was always fishing about in the pot for the best piece of meat, and if there was but one partridge shot, he would try to roast it for himself. If there was any delicacy he wanted more than his share." Things assume such different proportions in the wilds; after two months living on palm-tree tops and monkeys, a ten-cent can of condensed milk bought for three dollars from a rubber explorer far exceeds in value the greatest delicacy of the season to the ordinary citizen who has a varied and sufficient menu at his command every day in the year.

Even as small children father held us responsible to the law of the jungle. He would take us out on camping trips to a neck of land four or five miles across the bay from home. We would row there in the afternoon, the boats laden with blankets and food. Then we would make a driftwood fire on which to fry our supper—usually bacon and chicken. I do not know whether it was the, to us, wild romance of our position, or the keen appetite from the row, but never since then have I eaten such bacon. Not even the smallest child was allowed to show a disposition to grab, or select his pieces of chicken—we were taught that that was an unpardonable offense out camping, and might cause the culprit to be left behind next time. And woe to any one who in clumsily walking about kicked sand into the frying-pan. After supper we would heap more drift-wood on the fire, and drape ourselves in our blankets. Then we would stretch ourselves out in the sand while father would tell us ghost stories. The smallest of us lay within reach of father where we could touch him if the story became too vivid for our nerves and we needed the reassuring feel of his clothes to bring us back to reality. There was, however, a delicious danger in being too near him. In stories in which the "haunt" seized his victim, father generally illus-trated the action by making a grab at the nearest child. After the stories were finished we rolled up in our blankets and, thoroughly permeated with sand, we slept until the first faint light of dawn. Then there was the fire to be built up, and the breakfast cooked, and the long row home. As we rowed we chanted a ballad, usually of a seafaring nature; it might be "The Rhyme of the Three Sealers," or "The Galley Slave," or "Simon Danz." Father taught us these and many more, *viva voce*, when he was dressing for dinner. A child was not taken along on these "campings out" until he was six or seven. They took place three or four times a summer, and con-tinued until after the African expedition. By that time we were most of us away at work, scattered far and wide.

Father always threw himself into our plays and romps when we were small as if he were no older than ourselves, and with all that he had seen and done and gone through, there was never any one with so fresh and enthusiastic an attitude. His wonderful versatility and his enormous power of concentration and absorption were unequalled. He could turn from the consideration of the most grave problems of state to romp with us children as if there were not a worry in the world. Equally could he bury himself in an exhaustive treatise on the *History of the Mongols* or in the *Hound of the Baskervilles.*

Until father sold his ranches in North Dakota he used to go out West each year for a month or so. Unfortunately, we were none of us old enough to be taken along, but we would wait eagerly for his letters, and the recipient of what we called a picture letter gloried in the envy of the rest until another mail placed a substitute upon the pedestal. In these picture letters father would sketch scenes and incidents about the ranch or on his short hunting trips. We read most of them to pieces, unluckily, but the other day I came across one of the non-picture letters that father wrote me:

> August 30, '96.
> Out on the prairie.
>
> I must send my little son a letter too, for his father loves him very much. I have just ridden into camp on Muley,[1] with a prongbuck strapped behind the saddle; I was out six hours before shooting it. Then we all sat down on the ground in the shade of the wagon and had dinner, and now I shall clean my gun, and then go and take a bath in a big pool nearby, where there is a large flat stone on the edge, so I don't have to get my feet muddy. I sleep in the buffalo hide bag and I never take my clothes off when I go to bed!

By the time we were twelve or thirteen we were encouraged to plan hunting trips in the West. Father never had time to go with us, but we would be sent out to some friend of his, like Captain Seth Bullock, to spend two or three weeks in the Black Hills, or perhaps we would go after duck and prairie-chicken with Marvin Hewitt. Father would enter into all the plans and go down with us to the range to practise with rifle or shotgun, and when we came back we would go over every detail of the trip with him, revelling in his praise when he felt that we had acquitted ourselves well.

Father was ever careful to correct statements to the effect that he was a crack shot. He would explain how little being one had to do with success and achievement as a hunter. Perseverance, skill in tracking, quick vision, endurance, stamina, and a cool head, coupled with average ability as a marksman, produced far greater results than mere skill with a rifle—unaccompanied to any marked extent by the other attributes. It was the sum of all these qualities, each above the average, but none emphasized to an extraordinary degree, that accounted for father's great success in the hunting-field. He would point out many an excellent shot at a target who was of no use against game. Sometimes this would be due to lack of nerve. Father himself was equally cool and unconcerned whether his quarry was a charging lion or a jack-rabbit; with, when it came to the question of scoring a hit, the resultant advantage in the size of the former as a target. In other instances a good man at the range was not so good in the field because he was accustomed to shooting under conventional and regulated conditions, and fell down when it came to shooting under disadvantageous circumstances—if he had been running and were winded, if he were hungry or wet, or tired, or feeling the sun, if he were uncertain of the wind or the range. Sometimes, of course, a crack shot possesses all the other qualities; such is the case with Stewart Edward White, whom Cuninghame classified as the best shot with whom he had hunted in all his twenty-five years in the wilds. Father shot on a par with Cuninghame, and a good deal better than I, though not as well as Tarleton.

I have often heard father regret the fact that he did not care for shooting with the shotgun. He pointed out that it was naturally the most accessible and least expensive form of hunting. His eyesight made it almost impossible for him to attain much skill with a shotgun, and although as a boy and young man he went off after duck for sport, in later years he never used a shotgun except for collecting specimens or shooting for the pot. He continually encouraged us to learn to shoot with the gun. In a letter he wrote me to Europe when I was off after chamois he said: "I have played tennis a little with both Archie and Quentin, and have shot with the rifle with Archie and seen that he has practised shotgun shooting with Seaman."

When my brother and myself were ten and eight, respectively, father took us and four of our cousins of approximately the same ages to the Great South Bay for a cruise, with some fishing and bird-shooting thrown in, as the guest of Regis Post. It was a genuine sacrifice on father's part, for he loathed sailing, detested fishing, and was, to say the least, lukewarm about bird-shooting. Rowing was the only method of progression by water for which he cared. The trip was a great success, however, and father enjoyed it more than he anticipated, for with the help of our host he instructed us in caring for ourselves and our firearms. I had a venerable 12-bore pin-fire gun which was the first weapon my father ever owned. It was usually known in the family as the "rust bore" because in the course of its eventful career it had become so pitted and scarred with rust that you could put in as much time as you wished cleaning and oiling without the slightest effect. I stood in no little awe of the pin-fire because of its recoil when fired, and as I was in addition a miserably poor shot, my bag on the Great South Bay trip was not large. It consisted of one reedbird, which father with infinite pains and determination at length succeeded in enabling me to shoot. I am sure he never spent more time and effort on the most difficult stalk after some coveted trophy in the West or in Africa.

Father's hunting experiences had been confined to the United States, but he had taken especial interest in reading about Africa, the sportsman's paradise. When we were small he would read us incidents from the hunting books of Roualeyn Gordon Cumming, or Samuel Baker, or Drummond, or Baldwin. These we always referred to as "I stories," because they were told in the first person, and when we were sent to bed we would clamor for just one more, a petition that was seldom denied. Before we were old enough to appreciate the adventures we were shown the pictures, and through Cornwallis Harris's beautiful colored prints in the *Portraits of Game and Wild Animals of Southern Africa* we soon learned to distinguish the great beasts of Africa. The younger Gordon Cumming came to stay with us at Sagamore, and when father would get him to tell us hunting incidents from his own varied career, we listened enthralled to a really living "I story." To us he was known as the "Elephant Man," from his prowess in the pursuit of the giant pachyderm.

Then there was also the "Shark Man." He was an Australian who told us most thrilling tales of encounters with sharks witnessed when among the pearl-divers. I remember vividly his description of seeing a shark attack one of the natives working for him. The man was pulled aboard only after the shark had bitten a great chunk from his side and exposed his heart, which they could see still beating. He said, "Master, master, big fish," before he died.

The illustrations in Millais's *Breath from the Veldt* filled us with delight, and to this day I know of no etching that affects me as does the frontispiece by the author's father. It is called the "Last Trek." An old hunter is lying dead beside his ox-wagon; near him squat two of his Kafir boys, and in the distance graze herds of zebra and hartebeeste and giraffe.

Of the mighty hunters that still survived at that time, father admired most Mr. F. C. Selous. His books he knew almost by heart. Whenever Selous came to the United States he would stay with us, and father would sit up till far into the night talking of wild life in the open. Selous, at sixty-five, enlisted in the late war as a private; he rose to be captain, and was decorated with the D. S. O. for gallantry, before he fell, fighting the Germans in East Africa. No one could have devised a more fitting end for the gallant old fellow than to die at the head of his men, in a victorious battle on those plains he had roamed so often and loved so well, fighting against the worst and most dangerous beast of his generation.

In 1887 father founded a hunting club called the "Boone and Crockett" after two of the most mighty hunters of America. No one was entitled to membership who had not brought down in fair chase three species of American big game. The membership was limited to a hundred and I well remember my father's pride when my brother and I qualified and were eventually elected members. The club interests itself particularly in the conservation of wild life, and the establishment of game refuges. Mr. Selous and other English hunters were among the associate members.

In the summer of 1908 my father told me that when his term in the White House ended the following spring, he planned to make a trip to Africa, and that if I wished to do so I could accompany him. There was no need to ask whether I wanted to go. At school when we were writing compositions, mine almost invariably took the form of some imaginary journey across the "Dark Continent." Still, father had ever made it a practice to talk to us as if we were contemporaries. He would never order or even tell us to follow a certain line; instead, he discussed it with us, and let us draw our own conclusions. In that way we felt that while we had his unreserved backing, we were yet acting on our own initiative, and were ourselves responsible for the results. If a boy is forced to do a thing he often makes but a half-hearted attempt to succeed, and lays his failure to the charge of the person who forced him, although he might well have come through with flying colors had he felt that he was acting on his own responsibility. In his discussions with us, father could of course shape our opinions in what he thought the proper mould.

In like manner, when it came to taking me to Africa father wanted me to go, but he also wanted me to thoroughly understand the pro's and con's. He explained to me that it was a holiday that he was allowing himself at fifty, after a very busy life—that if I went I would have to make up my mind that my holiday was coming at the beginning of my life, and be prepared to work doubly hard to justify both him and myself for having taken it. He said that the great danger lay in my being unsettled, but he felt that taken rightly the experience could be made a valuable asset instead of a liability. After we had once finished the discussion and settled that I was to go, father never referred to it again. He then set about preparing for the expedition. Mr. Edward North Buxton was another African hunter whom he greatly admired, and it was to him and to Selous that he chiefly turned for aid in making his plans. It was often said of father that he was hasty and inclined to go off at half-cock. There was never any one who was less so. He would gather his information and make his preparations with painstaking care, and then when the moment came to act he was thoroughly equipped and prepared to do so with that lightning speed that his enemies characterized as rash hot-headedness.

Father always claimed that it was by discounting and guarding against all possible causes of failure that he won his successes. His last great battle, that for preparedness for the part that "America the Unready" would have to play in the World War, was true to his life creed. For everything he laid his plans in advance, foreseeing as far as was humanly possible each contingency to be encountered.

For the African expedition he made ready in every way. I was at the time at Harvard, and almost every letter brought some reference to preparations. One day it would be: "The Winchester rifles came out for trial and all of them were sighted wrong. I sent them back with rather an acid letter." Then again: "You and I will be so rusty when we reach Sir Alfred Pease's ranch that our first efforts at shooting are certain to be very bad. In March we will practise at Oyster Bay with the 30-30 until we get what I would call the 'rifle sense' back again, and this will make it easier for us when, after a month's sea trip, we take up the business of hunting."

A group of thirty or forty of the most famous zoologists and sportsmen presented my father with a heavy, double-barrelled gun. "At last I have tried the double-barrelled Holland Elephant rifle. It is a perfect beauty and it shoots very accurately, but of course the recoil is tremendous, and I fired very few shots. I shall get you to fire it two or three times at a target after we reach Africa, just so that you shall be thoroughly familiar with it, if, or when, you use it after big game. There is no question that except under extraordinary circumstances it would be the best weapon for elephant, rhino, and buffalo. I think the 405 Winchester will be as good for everything else."

"About all my African things are ready now, or will be in a few days. I suppose yours are in good trim also [a surreptitious dig at a somewhat lackadaisical son.] I am pursuing my usual plan of taking all the precautions in advance."

A few days later came another reference to the Holland & Holland: "The double-barrelled four-fifty shot beautifully, but I was paralyzed at the directions which accompanied it to the effect that two shots must always be fired in the morning before starting, as otherwise from the freshly oiled barrels the first shot would go high. This is all nonsense and I shall simply have to see that the barrels are clean of the oil." The recoil of the big gun was so severe that it became a standing joke as to whether we did not fear it more than a charging elephant!

Father gave the closest attention to every detail of the equipment. The first provision lists prepared by his friends in England were drawn up on a presidential scale with champagne and pâté de foies gras and all sorts of luxuries. These were blue-pencilled and two American staples substituted—baked beans and canned tomatoes. Father always retained the appreciation of canned tomatoes gained in the early ranching days in the West. He would explain how delicious he had found it in the Bad Lands after eating the tomatoes to drink the juice from the can. In hunting in a temperate climate such as our West, a man can get along with but very little, and it is difficult to realize that a certain amount of luxury is necessary in the tropics to maintain oneself fit. Then, too, in Africa the question of transportation was fairly simple—and almost everywhere we were able to keep ourselves and the porters amply supplied with fresh meat. Four years later during the descent of the Duvida—the "River of Doubt"—we learned to our bitter cost what it meant to travel in the tropics as lightly equipped as one could, with but little hardship, in the north. It was not, however, through our own lack of forethought, but due rather to the necessities and shifting chances of a difficult and dangerous exploring expedition.

Even if it is true as Napoleon said, that an army marches on its belly, still, it won't go far unless its feet are properly shod, and since my father had a skin as tender as a baby's, he took every precaution that his boots should fit him properly and not rub. "The modified duffle-bags came all right. I suppose we will get the cotton-soled shoes, but I do not know. How do you like the rubber-soled shoes? Don't you think before ordering other pairs it would be as well to wait until you see the army shoes here, which are light and somehow look as if they were more the kind you ordinarily use? How many pairs have you now for the African trip, and how many more do you think you want?"

Father was fifty years old in the October before we left for Africa, and the varied experiences of his vigorous life had, as he used to say, battered and chipped him. One eye was to all intents useless from the effects of a boxing-match, and from birth he had been so astigmatic as to be absolutely unable to use a rifle and almost unable to find his way in the woods without his glasses. He never went off without eight or ten pairs so distributed throughout his kit as to minimize the possibility of being crippled through any ordinary accident. Even so, any one who has worn glasses in the tropics knows how easily they fog over, and how hopeless they are in the rains. It was a continual source of amazement to see how skilfully father had discounted this handicap in advance and appeared to be unhampered by it.

Another serious threat lay in the leg that had been injured when the carriage in which he was driving was run down by a trolley-car, and the secret service man with him was killed. In September, 1908, he wrote me from Washington: "I have never gotten over the effects of the trolley-car accident six years ago, when, as you will remember, they had to cut down to the shin bone. The shock permanently damaged the bone, and if anything happens there is always a chance of trouble which would be serious. Before I left Oyster Bay, while riding, I got a rap on the shin bone from a branch. This was either the cause or the occasion of an inflammation, which had grown so serious when I got back here that Doctor Rixey had to hastily take it in hand. For a couple of days it was uncertain whether we would not have to have another operation and remove some of the bones of the leg, but fortunately the doctor got it in hand all right, and moreover it has enabled me to learn just what I ought to do if I am threatened with similar trouble in Africa."

His activity, however, was little hampered by his leg, for a few weeks later he wrote: "I have done very little jumping myself, and that only of the small jumps up to four feet, because it is evident that I have got to be pretty careful of my leg, and that an accident of at all a serious character might throw me out of gear for the African trip. This afternoon by the way, Archie Butt and I took a scramble down Rock Creek. It was raining and the rocks were slippery, and at one point I slipped off into the creek, but merely bruised myself in entirely safe places, not hurting my leg at all. When we came to the final and stiffest cliff climb, it was so dark that Archie couldn't get up." From which it may be seen that neither endurance nor skill suffered as a result of the accident to the leg. Still, as Bret Harte says, "We always wink with the weaker eye," and when anything went wrong, the leg was sure to be implicated. Father suffered fearfully with it during the descent of the River of Doubt. One of the most constant pictures of father that I retain is at Sagamore after dinner on the piazza. He would draw his chair out from the roofed-over part to where he could see the moon and the stars. When things were black he would often quote Jasper Petulengro in Borrow's *Lavengro:* "Life is sweet, brother. . . . There's day and night, brother, both sweet things; sun, moon, and stars, all sweet things; . . . and likewise there's a wind on the heath," and would add: "Yes, there's always the wind on the heath." From where he sat he looked across the fields to the dark woods, and over the tree-tops to the bay with the changing twinkling lights of the small craft; across the bay to the string of lamps along the causeway leading to Centre Island, and beyond that again Long Island Sound with occasionally a "tall Fall Steamer light." For a while father would drink his coffee in silence, and then his rocking-chair would start creaking and he would say: "Do you remember that night in the Sotik when the gunbearers were skinning the big lion?" or "What a lovely camp that was under the big tree in the Lado when we were hunting the giant eland?"

We get three sorts and periods of enjoyment out of a hunting trip. The first is when the plans are being discussed and the outfit assembled; this is the pleasure of anticipation. The second is the enjoyment of the actual trip itself; and the third is the pleasure of retrospection when we sit round a blazing wood-fire and talk over the incidents and adventures of the trip. There is no general rule to know which of the three gives the keenest joy. I can think of a different expedition in which each sort stands out in pre-eminence. Even if the trip has been exceptionally hard and the luck unusually bad, the pleasures of anticipation and preparation cannot be taken away, and frequently the retrospect is the more satisfactory because of the difficulties and discomforts surmounted.

I think we enjoyed the African trip most in the actuality, and that is saying a great deal. It was a wonderful "adventure" and all the world seemed young. Father has quoted in the foreword to *African Game Trails:* "I speak of Africa and golden joys." It was a line that I have heard him repeat to himself many times. In Africa everything was new. He revelled in the vast plains blackened with herds of grazing antelope. From his exhaustive reading and retentive memory he knew already the history and the habits of the different species of game. When we left camp in the early morning we never could foretell what we would run into by nightfall—we were prepared for anything from an elephant to a dik-dik—the graceful diminutive antelope no larger than a hare. In the evening, after we had eaten we would gather round the camp-fire —for in the highlands the evenings were chilly—and each would tell the adventures of his day, and discuss plans for the morrow. Then we would start paralleling and comparing. Father would

Sir Alfred Pease's sketch of our first giraffe hunt

illustrate with adventures of the old days in our West; Cuninghame from the lore gathered during his twenty years in Africa would relate some anecdote, and Mearns would talk of life among the wild tribes in the Philippines.

Colonel Mearns belonged to the medical corps in the army. He had come with us as an ornithologist, for throughout his military career he had been actively interested in sending specimens from wherever he was serving to the Smithsonian National Museum in Washington. His mild manner belied his fearless and intrepid disposition. A member of the expedition once came into camp with an account of the doctor, whom he had just run across—looking too benevolent for this world, engaged in what our companion described as "slaughtering humming-birds, pursuing them from bush to bush." One of his Philippine adventures filled us with a delighted interest for which I don't believe he fully appreciated the reason. He told us how with a small force he had been hemmed in by a large number of Moros. The Americans took refuge in a stockade on a hilltop. The Moros advanced time and again with the greatest gallantry, and Mearns explained how sorry he felt for them as they fell—some under the very walls of the stockade. In a musing tone at the end he added: "I slipped out of the stockade that night and collected a most interesting series of skulls; they're in the Smithsonian to-day."

Father was the rare combination of a born raconteur—with the gift of putting in all the little details that make a story—and an equally good listener. He was an adept at drawing people out. His interest was so whole-hearted and obvious that the shyest, most tongue-tied adventurer found himself speaking with entire freedom. Every one with whom we came in contact fell under the charm. Father invariably thought the best of a person, and for that very reason every one was at his best with him—and felt bound to justify his confidence and judgment. With him I always thought of the Scotch story of the MacGregor who, when a friend told him that it was an outrage that at a certain banquet he should have been given a seat half-way down the table, replied: "Where the

MacGregor sits is the head of the table!" Where father sat was always the head of the table, and yet he treated every one with the same courtesy and simplicity, whether it was the governor of the Protectorate or the poorest Boer settler. I remember how amazed some were at the lack of formality in his relationship with the members of the expedition. Many people who have held high positions feel it incumbent on them to maintain a certain distance in their dealings with their less illustrious fellow men. If they let down the barrier they feel, they would lose dignity. They are generally right, for their superiority is not innate, but the result of chance. With father it was otherwise. The respect and consideration felt for him could not have been greater, and would certainly not have been so sincere, had he built a seven-foot barrier about himself.

He was most essentially unselfish, and wanted no more than would have been his just due if the expedition, instead of being owing entirely to him, both financially and otherwise, had been planned and carried out by all of us. He was a natural champion of the cause of every man, and not only in his books would he carefully give credit where it was due, but he would endeavor to bring about recognition through outside channels. Thus he felt that Colonel Rondon deserved wide acknowledgment for the years of exploring in the Brazilian Hinterland; and he brought it to the attention of the American and British Geographical Societies. As a result, the former awarded the gold medal to Colonel Rondon. In the same way father championed the cause of the naturalists who went with him on his expeditions. He did his best to see that the museums to which they belonged should appreciate their services, and give them the opportunity to follow the results through. When an expedition brings back material that has not been described, the museum publishes pamphlets listing the new species, and explaining their habitats and characteristics. This is rarely done by the man who did the actual collecting. Father, whenever it was feasible, arranged for the naturalists who had accompanied or taken part in the collecting to have the credit of writing the pamphlets describing the results of their work. To a layman this would not seem much, but in reality it means a great deal. Father did all he could to encourage his companions to write their experiences, for most of them had led eventful lives filled with unusual incident. When, as is often the case, the actor did not have the power of written narrative, father would be the first to recognize it, and knew that if inadequately described, the most eventful careers may be of no more interest than the catalogue of ships in the *Odyssey*, or the "begat" chapters in the Bible. If, however, father felt that there existed a genuine ability to write, he would spare no efforts to place the articles; in some cases he would write introductions, and in others, reviews of the book, if the results attained to that proportion.

One of the most careful preparations that father made for the African expedition was the choosing of the library. He selected as wide a range as possible, getting the smallest copy of each book that was obtainable with decent reading type. He wanted a certain number of volumes mainly for the contrast to the daily life. He told me that he had particularly enjoyed Swinburne and Shelley in ranching days in the Bad Lands, because they were so totally foreign to the life and the country —and supplied an excellent antidote to the daily round. Father read so rapidly that he had to plan very carefully in order to have enough books to last him through a trip. He liked to have a mixture of serious and light literature—chaff, as he called the latter. When he had been reading histories and scientific discussions and political treatises for a certain length of time, he would plunge into an orgy of detective stories and novels about people cast away on desert islands.

The plans for the Brazilian expedition came into being so unexpectedly that he could not choose his library with the usual care. He brought Gibbon's *Decline and Fall of the Roman Empire* in the Everyman's edition, and farmed out a volume to each of us, and most satisfactory it proved to all. He also brought *Marcus Aurelius* and *Epictetus*, but when he tried to read them during the descent of the Rio da Duvida, they only served to fill him with indignation at their futility. Some translations of Greek plays, not those of Gilbert Murray, for which he had unstinted praise, met with but little better success, and we were nearly as badly off for reading matter as we were for provisions. I had brought along a selection of Portuguese classics and a number of French novels. The former were useless to father, but Henri Bordeaux and Maurice Leblanc were grist to the mill. It was father's first introduction to Arsène, and he thoroughly enjoyed it—he liked the style, although for matter he preferred Conan Doyle. Father never cared very much about French novels—the French books that he read most were scientific volumes—histories of the Mongols—and an occasional hunting book, but he afterward became a great admirer of Henri Bordeaux.

At last the time came when there was nothing left but the Oxford books of English and French verse. The one of English verse he had always disliked. He said that if there were to be any American poetry included, it should be at any rate a good selection. The choice from Longfellow's poems appealed to him as particularly poor, and I think that it was for this reason that he disapproved of the whole collection. Be that as it may, I realized how hard up for something to read father must be when he asked me for my Oxford book of English verse. For French verse father had never cared. He said it didn't sing sufficiently. "The Song of Roland" was the one exception he granted. It was, therefore, a still greater proof of distress when he borrowed the Oxford book of French verse. He always loved to tell afterward that when he first borrowed it he started criticising and I had threatened to take it away if he continued to assail my favorites. In spite of all this he found it infinitely preferable to *Epictetus* and *Marcus Aurelius*, and, indeed, became very fond of some of the selections. Villon and Ronsard particularly interested him.

When riding along through the wilderness father would often repeat poetry to himself. To learn a poem he had only to read it through a few times, and he seemed never to forget it. Sometimes we would repeat the poem together. It might be parts of the "Saga of King Olaf," or Kipling's "Rhyme of the Three Sealers," or "Grave of a Hundred Head," or, perhaps, "The Bell Buoy"—or again it might be something from Swinburne or Shelley or Keats—or the "Ballad of Judas Iscariot." He was above all fond of the poetry of the open, and I think we children got much of our love for the outdoor life, not only from actual example, but from the poetry that father taught us.

There was an indissoluble bond between him and any of his old hunting companions, and in no matter what part of the world he met them, all else was temporarily forgotten in the eager exchange of reminiscences of old days. On the return from Africa, Seth Bullock, of Deadwood, met us in London. How delighted father was to see him, and how he enjoyed the captain's comments on England and things English! One of the captain's first remarks on reaching London was to the effect that he was so glad to see father that he felt like hanging his hat on the dome of Saint Paul's and shooting it off. We were reminded of Artemus Ward's classic reply to the guard who found him tapping, with his cane, an inscription in Westminster Abbey: "Come, come, sir, you mustn't do that. It isn't permitted, you know!" Whereupon Artemus Ward turned upon him: "What, mustn't do it? If I like it, I'll buy it!" It was never difficult to trail the captain. When my sister and I were going through Edinburgh Castle, the local guide showed us an ancient gun, firing a cluster of five or six barrels. With great amusement he told us how an American to whom he was showing the piece a few days previously had remarked that to be shot at with that gun must be like taking a shower-bath. A few questions served to justify the conclusion we had immediately formed as to the identity of our predecessor. Father had him invited to the dinner given by the donors of the Holland & Holland elephant rifle.

Of the hunting comrades of his early days, he told me that Mr. R. H. Munro Ferguson was the most satisfactory of all, for he met all requirements—always good-humored when things went wrong, possessing a keen sense of humor, understanding the value of silent companionship, and so well read and informed as to be able to discuss appreciatively any of the multitudinous questions of literature or world affairs that interested my father.

In Washington when an old companion turned up he would be triumphantly borne off to lunch, to find himself surrounded by famous scientists, authors, senators, and foreign diplomats. Father would shift with lightning rapidity from one to the other—first he might be discussing some question of Indian policy and administration, next the attitude of a foreign power—then an author's latest novel—and a few moments later, he would have led on Johnny Goff to telling an experience with the cougar hounds.

Any man who had hunted with father was ready to follow him to the ends of the earth, and no passage of time could diminish his loyalty. With father the personal equation counted for so much. He was so wholeheartedly interested in his companions—in their aspirations and achievements. In every detail he was keenly interested, and he would select from his library those volumes which he thought would most interest each companion, and, perhaps, develop in him the love of the wonderful avocation which he himself found in reading. His efforts were not always crowned with success. Father felt that our African companion, R. J. Cuninghame, the "Bearded Master," as the natives called him, being Scotch should be interested in Scott's novels, so he selected from the "Pigskin Library" a copy of one of them— *Waverley*, I think it was. For some weeks Cuninghame made progress, not rapid, it is true, for he confessed to finding the notes the most interesting part of the book, then one day when they were sitting under a tree together in a rest during the noonday heat, and father in accordance with his invariable custom took out a book from his saddle-pocket, R. J. produced *Waverley* and started industriously to work on it. Father looked over his shoulder to see where he had got to, and to his amused delight found that Cuninghame had been losing ground—he was three chapters farther back than he had been two weeks before!

Father and R. H. Munro Ferguson at the Elkhorn Ranch, after the return from a successful hunting trip

We more than once had occasion to realize how largely the setting is responsible for much that we enjoy in the wilds. Father had told me of how he used to describe the bellowing of the bull elk as he would hear it ring out in the frozen stillness of the forests of Wyoming. He thought of it, and talked of it, as a weird, romantic call—until one day when he was walking through the zoological gardens accompanied by the very person to whom he had so often given the description. As they passed the wapitis' enclosure, a bull bellowed, and father's illusions and credit were simultaneously shattered, for the romantic call he had so often dwelt upon was, in a zoological park, nothing more than a loud and discordant sort of bray.

In spite of this lesson we would see something among the natives that was interesting or unusual and get it to bring home, only to find that it was the exotic surroundings that had been responsible for a totally fictitious charm. A wild hill tribe in Africa use anklets made from the skin of the colobus, a graceful, long-haired monkey colored black and white. When father produced the anklets at home, the only thing really noticeable about them was the fact that they smelt!

Another equally unfortunate case was the affair of the beehives. The same hill tribe was very partial to honey. An individual's wealth was computed in the number of beehives that he possessed. They were made out of hollowed logs three or four feet long and eight or ten inches in diameter. A wife or a cow was bought for an agreed upon number of beehives, and when we were hunting, no matter how hot the trail might be, the native tracker would, if we came to a clearing and saw some bees hovering about the forest flowers, halt and offer up a prayer that the bees should deposit the honey in one of his hives. It seemed natural to bring a hive home, but viewed in the uncompromising light of the North Shore of Long Island it was merely a characterless, uninteresting log.

Not the least of the many delights of being a hunting companion of father's was his humor. No one could tell a better story, whether it was what he used to call one of his "old grouse in the gunroom" stories, or an account, with sidelights, of a contemporaneous adventure. The former had to do with incidents in his early career in the cow-camps of the Dakotas, or later on with the regiment in Cuba—and phrases and incidents of them soon became coin-current in the expedition. Father's humor was never under any circumstances ill-natured, or of such a sort as might make its object feel uncomfortable. If anything amusing occurred to a member of the expedition, father would embroider the happening in inimitable fashion, but always in such a way that the victim himself was the person most amused. The accompanying drawing will serve as illustration. Father and I had gone out to get some buck to eke out the food-supply for the porters. We separated, but some time later I caught sight of father and thought I would join him and return to camp. I didn't pay particular attention to what he was doing, and as he was some way off I failed to notice that he was walking stooped to keep concealed by a rise of ground from some buck he was stalking. The result was the picture.

Before we started on the serious exploring part of the Brazilian trip, we paid visits to several fazendas or ranches in the state of Matto Grosso, with the purpose of hunting jaguar, as well as the lesser game of the country. One of the fazendas at which we stayed belonged to the governor of the state. When we were wakened before daylight to start off on the hunt we were given, in Brazilian fashion, the small cup of black coffee and piece of bread which constitutes the native Brazilian breakfast. We would then sally forth to return to the ranch not before noon, and sometimes much later, as the hunting luck dictated. We would find an enormous lunch waiting for us at the house. Father, who was accustomed to an American breakfast, remarked regretfully that he wished the lunch were divided, or that at least part of it were used to supplement the black coffee of daybreak. The second morning, as I went down the hall, the dining-room door was ajar, and I caught sight of the table laden with the cold meats and salads that were to serve as part of our elaborate luncheon many dim hours hence. I hurried back to tell father, and we tip-

An Elderly Parent, in the temporary absence of his Affectionate son, begins a Cautious Stalk of a buck.

Joyful Emotions of the Aff. son, and the Aff. son's followers, on witnessing the Cautious Stalk and preparing to take an Active Part in it.

Arrival of Aff. son; mixed emotions of Elderly Parent; buck in vanishing perspective.

Facsimile of a picture letter by father

toed cautiously into the dining-room, closing the door noiselessly behind us. While we were engaged in making rapid despatch of a cold chicken, we heard our hosts calling, and the next minute the head of the house popped in the door! As father said afterward, we felt and looked like two small boys caught stealing jam in the pantry.

The Brazilian exploration was not so carefully planned as the African trip, because father had not intended to make much of an expedition. The first time he mentioned the idea was in April, 1913, in reply to a letter I wrote from São Paulo describing a short hunting expedition that I had made. "The forest must be lovely; some time I must get down to see you, and we'll take a fortnight's outing, and you shall hunt and I'll act as what in the North Woods we used to call 'Wangan man,' and keep camp!"

Four mouths later he wrote that he was planning to come down and see me; that he had been asked to make addresses in Brazil, Argentina, and Chile, and "I shall take a naturalist with me, if, as I hope, I return via Paraguay and the Amazon." At the time it did not look as if it would be possible for me to go on the trip. In father's next letter he said that after he left me, "instead of returning in the ordinary tourist Bryan-Bryce-way, I am going to see if it is possible to work across from the Plata into the valley of the Amazon, and come out through the Brazilian forest. This may not be possible. It won't be anything like our African trip. There will be no hunting and no adventures, so that I shall not have the pang I otherwise would about not taking you along." These plans were amplified and extended a certain amount, but in the last letter I received they didn't include a very serious expedition.

"I shall take the Springfield and the Fox on my trip, but I shall not expect to do any game-shooting. I think it would need the Bwana Merodadi, [My name among the natives in Africa] and not his stout and rheumatic elderly parent to do hunting in the Brazilian forest. I shall have a couple of naturalists with me of the Heller stamp, and I shall hope to get a fair collection for the New York Museum—Fairfield Osborn's museum."

It was at Rio that father first heard of the River of Doubt. Colonel Rondon in an exploring expedition had crossed a large river and no one knew where it went to. Father felt that to build dugouts and descend the river offered a chance to accomplish some genuine and interesting exploration. It was more of a trip than he had planned for, but the Brazilian Government arranged for Colonel Rondon to make up an accompanying expedition.

When father went off into the wilds he was apt to be worried until he had done something which would in his mind justify the expedition and relieve it from the danger of being a fiasco. In Africa he wished to get at least one specimen each of the four great prizes—the lion, the elephant, the buffalo, and the rhinoceros. It was the lion for which he was most keen—and which he also felt was the most problematical. Luck was with us, and we had not been hunting many days before father's ambition was fulfilled. It was something that he had long desired—indeed it is the pinnacle of most hunters' ambitions—so it was a happy cavalcade that rode back to camp in the wake of the natives that were carrying the lioness slung on a long pole. The blacks were chanting a native song of triumph, and father was singing "Whack-fa-lal for Lannigan's Ball," as a sort of "chant pagan."

Father was more fluent than exact in expressing himself in foreign languages. As he himself said of his French, he spoke it "as if it were a non-Aryan tongue, having neither gender nor tense." He would, however, always manage to make himself understood, and never seemed to experience any difficulty in understanding his interlocutor. In Africa he had a most complicated combination of sign-language and coined words, and though I could rarely make out what he and his gun-bearer were talking about, they never appeared to have any difficulty in understanding each other. Father could read Spanish, and he had not been in Brazil long before he could make out the trend of any conversation in Portuguese. With the Brazilians he always spoke French, or, on rare occasions, German.

Putting the tape on a tusker

Reading from left to right: unknown gun-bearer, Kasitura, Father, Juma Johari, Tarlton, Cuninghame

He was most conscientious about his writing. Almost every day when he came in from hunting he would settle down to work on the articles that were from time to time sent back to *Scribner's.* This daily task was far more onerous than any one who has not tried it can imagine. When you come in from a long day's tramping, you feel most uninclined to concentrate on writing a careful and interesting account of the day's activities. Father was invariably good-humored about it, saying that he was paying for his fun. In Brazil when the mosquitoes and sand-flies were intolerable, he used to be forced to write swathed in a mosquito veil and with long gauntlets to protect hands and wrists.

During the descent of the River of Doubt in Brazil there were many black moments. It was impossible to hazard a guess within a month or more as to when we would get through to the Amazon. We had dugout canoes, and when we came to serious rapids or waterfalls we were forced to cut a trail around to the quiet water below. Then we must make a corduroy road with the trunks of trees over which to haul the dugouts. All this took a long time, and in some places where the river ran through gorges it was almost impossible. We lost in all six of the ten canoes with which we started, and of course much of our food-supply and general equipment. It was necessary to delay and build two more canoes—a doubly laborious task because of the axes and adzes which had gone down in the shipwrecks. The Brazil nuts upon which we had been counting to help out our food-supply had had an off year. If this had not been so we would have fared by no means badly, for these nuts may be ground into flour or roasted or prepared in a number of different ways. Another source upon which we counted failed us when we found that there were scarcely any fish in the river. For some inexplicable reason many of the tributaries of the Amazon teem with fish, while others flowing through similar country and under parallel conditions contain practically none. We went first onto half rations, and then were forced to still further reduce the issue. We had only the clothes in which we stood and were wet all day and slept wet throughout the night. There would be a heavy down-pour, then out would come the sun and we would be steamed dry, only to be drenched once more a half-hour later.

Working waist-deep in the water in an attempt to dislodge a canoe that had been thrown upon some rocks out in the stream, father slipped, and, of course, it was his weak leg that suffered. Then he came down with fever, and in his weakened condition was attacked with a veritable plague of deep abscesses. It can be readily understood that the entourage and environment were about as unsuitable for a sick man as any that could be imagined. Nothing but father's indomitable spirit brought him through. He was not to be downed by anything, although he knew well that the chances were against his coming out. He made up his mind that as long as he could, he would go along, but that once he could no longer travel, and held up the expedition, he would arrange for us to go on without him. Of course he did not at the time tell us this, but he reasoned that with our very limited supply of provisions, and the impossibility of living on the country, if the expedition halted it would not only be of no avail as far as he was concerned, but the chances would be strongly in favor of no one coming through. With it all he was invariably cheerful, and in the blackest times ever ready with a joke. Sick as he was, he gave no one any trouble. He would walk slowly over the portages, resting every little while, and when the fever was not too severe we would, when we reached the farther end with the canoes, find him sitting propped against a tree reading a volume of Gibbon, or perhaps the Oxford book of verse.

There was one particularly black night; one of our best men had been shot and killed by a useless devil who escaped into the jungle, where he was undoubtedly killed by the Indians. We had been working through a series of rapids that seemed interminable. There would be a long carry, a mile or so clear going, and then more rapids. The fever was high and father was out of his head. Doctor Cajazeira, who was one of the three Brazilians with us, divided with me the watch during the night. The scene is vivid

Launching a newly made dugout on the Dúvida

before me. The black rushing river with the great trees towering high above along the bank; the sodden earth under foot; for a few moments the stars would be shining, and then the sky would cloud over and the rain would fall in torrents, shutting out sky and trees and river. Father first began with poetry; over and over again he repeated "In Xanadu did Kubla Khan a stately pleasure dome decree," then he started talking at random, but gradually he centred down to the question of supplies, which was, of course, occupying every one's mind. Part of the time he knew that I was there, and he would then ask me if I thought Cherrie had had enough to eat to keep going. Then he would forget my presence and keep saying to himself: "I can't work now, so I don't need much food, but he and Cherrie have worked all day with the canoes, they must have part of mine." Then he would again realize my presence and question me as to just how much Cherrie had had. How good faithful Cajazeira waked I do not know, but when his watch was due I felt him tap me on the shoulder, and crawled into my soggy hammock to sleep the sleep of the dead.

Father's courage was an inspiration never to be forgotten by any of us; without a murmur he would lie while Cajazeira lanced and drained the abscesses. When we got down beyond the rapids the river widened so that instead of seeing the sun through the canyon of the trees for but a few hours each day, it hung above us all the day like a molten ball and broiled us as if the river were a grid on which we were made fast. To a sick man it must have been intolerable.

It is when one is sick that one really longs for home. Lying in a hammock all unwashed and unshaven, suffocating beneath a mosquito-net, or tortured by mosquitoes and sand-flies when one raises the net to let in a breath of air—it is then that one dreams of clean pajamas and cool sheets and iced water. I have often heard father say when he was having a bout of fever at home, that it was almost a pleasure to be ill, particularly when you thought of all the past discomforts of fever in the wilds.

Father's disappointment at not being able to take a physical part in the war—as he has said, "to pay with his body for his soul's desire"—was bitter. Strongly as he felt about going, I doubt if his disappointment was much more keen than that of the British and French statesmen and generals, who so readily realized what his presence would mean to the Allied cause, and more than once requested in Washington that he be sent. Marshal Joffre made such a request in person, meeting with the usual evasive reply. Father took his disappointment as he had taken many another in his life, without letting it harm his usefulness, or discourage his aggressive energy. "In the fell clutch of circumstance he did not wince or cry aloud." Indeed, the whole of Henley's poem might well apply to father if it were possible to eliminate from it the unfortunate marring undercurrent of braggadocio with which father's attitude was never for an instant tinged. With the indomitable courage that knew no deterrent he continued to fight his battle on this side to make America's entry no empty action, as it threatened to be. He wrote me that he had hoped that I would be with him in this greatest adventure of all, but that since it was not to be, he could only be thankful that his four boys were per-mitted to do their part in the actual fighting.

When in a little town in Germany my brother and I got news of my father's death, there kept running through my head with monotonous insistency Kipling's lines:

"He scarce had need to doff his pride,
　Or slough the dress of earth,
　E'en as he trod that day to God
　So walked he from his birth,
　In simpleness and gentleness and honor and clean mirth."

That was my father, to whose comradeship and guidance so many of us look forward in the Happy Hunting-Grounds.

CHAPTER II

IN QUEST OF SABLE ANTELOPE

IT was a bright, sunny day toward the end of October, and I was walking along the streets of the old Portuguese town of Mombasa on the east coast of Equatorial Africa. Behind me, in ragged formation, marched some twenty-five blacks, all but four of them with loads on their heads; the four were my personal "boys," two gunbearers, a cook, and a tent-boy. They were scattered among the crowd, hurrying up those that tried to lag behind for a last farewell to the wives and sweethearts who were following along on either side, clad in the dark-blue or more gaudily colored sheets that served them for clothes.

At length our heterogeneous assembly reached the white sands of the harbor, and amid much confusion we stowed away into a couple of long, broad dugouts and were ferried out to a dhow that lay moored not far from the shore. We set sail amid the shrill cries of the women and a crowd of small children who, on our approach, had scurried out of the water like so many black monitor lizards.

We steered out across the bay toward a headland some two miles distant. There was just enough breeze to ruffle the water, but the dhow sped along at a rate that belied appearances. Sprawling among their loads the men lit cigarettes and chatted and joked, talking of the prospects of the trip, or the recent gossip of Mombasa. The sailors, not knowing that I understood Swahili, began to discuss me in loud tones. An awkward silence fell upon the porters, who didn't quite know how to tell them. Mali, my tent-boy, who was sitting near me, looked toward me and smiled. When the discussion became a little too personal, I turned to him and made a few pertinent remarks about the crew. The porters grinned delightedly, and rarely have I seen more shamefaced men than those sailors.

In far too short a time for all of us the dhow grounded on the other side and we jumped out and started to unload. A giant baobab-tree stood near the beach; a cluster of huts beneath it were occupied by some Swahilis who fished, and ran a small store, where my porters laid in a final supply of delicacies—sugar and tobacco.

It is customary to have a native head man, but on this short trip I had decided to do without one, for though the porters were new, my personal boys were old friends. Accordingly, when all the loads were ready and neatly arranged in line, I shouted "Bandika!" Great muscular black arms caught the packs and swung them up into place on the head, and off we started, along the old coast trail, worn deep with the traffic of centuries, and leading on for several hundred miles with native villages strung along its length. Behind me strode my two gun boys, then came the porters, all in single file, their present regular order a strong contrast with our disordered progress through the streets of Mombasa. Mali and Kombo, the cook, brought up the rear to look out for stragglers, and help unfortunates to rearrange their loads more comfortably.

A little way from the shore we passed an old Arab well; some women were drawing water from it, but at our approach they deserted their earthen jars and hurried away with shrill ejaculations. Fresh from the more arid interior, I imagined that the men would fill their gourds, but they filed past without stopping, for this was a land of many streams.

We continued on our way silently, now through stretches of sandy land covered with stunted bushes, now through native shambas, or cultivated fields, until we came upon a group of

A relic of the Portuguese occupation; an old well beside the trail

natives seated under a gigantic wide-spreading tree. It was a road-side shop, and the porters threw down their loads and shouldered their way to where the shopkeeper was squatting behind his wares —nuts, tobacco, tea, bits of brass wire, beads, and sweetmeats of a somewhat gruesome appearance. He was a striking-looking old fellow with a short gray beard. Pretty soon he came to where I was sitting with a measure of nuts for the white man; so in return I took out my tobacco-pouch and presented him with some of the white man's tobacco.

After a few minutes' rest we set out again and marched along for some time until we came to a cocoanut-palm grove, where I decided to camp for the night. The natives we were among were called the WaNyika—the "children of the wilderness."

Leaving the men to arrange camp under the supervision of the gun-bearers, I strolled over to a near-by village where there was a dance in full swing. The men were regaling themselves with cocoanut-wine, an evil-tasting liquid, made from fermented cocoanut-milk, they told me. The moon, almost at full, was rising when I returned to camp, and after supper I sat and smoked and watched "the night and the palms in the moonlight," until the local chief, or Sultani, as they called him, came up and presented me with some ripe cocoanuts, and sitting down on the ground beside me he puffed away at his long clay pipe, coughing and choking over the strong tobacco I had given him, but apparently enjoying it all immensely. When he left I remained alone, unable for some time to make up my mind to go to bed, such was the spell of the tropic moonlight and the distant half-heard songs of the dancing "children of the wilderness."

Early next morning we were on our way, and that night were camped a few hundred yards from the village of a grizzled old Sultani, whose domains lay in the heart of the sable country, for it was in search of these handsome antelopes that I had come. In southern Africa the adult males of the species are almost black, with white bellies, but here they were not so dark in color, resembling more nearly the southern female sable, which is a dark reddish brown. Both sexes carry long horns that sweep back in a graceful curve over the shoulders, those of the male much heavier and longer, sometimes, in the south, attaining five feet in length. The sable antelope is a savage animal, and when provoked, will attack man or beast. The rapier-like horns prove an effective weapon as many a dog has learned to its cost.

My tent was pitched beneath one of the large shade-trees in which the country abounds. This one was the village council-tree, and when I arrived the old men were seated beneath it on little wooden stools. These were each hacked out of a single log and were only five or six inches high. The owner carried his stool with him wherever he went, slinging it over his shoulder on a bit of rawhide or a chain.

There was trouble in the village, for after the first formal greetings were over the old chief told me that one of his sons had just died. There was about to be held a dance in his memory, and he led me over to watch it. We arrived just as the ceremony was starting. Only small boys were taking part in it, and it was anything but a mournful affair, for each boy had strung round his ankles baskets filled with pebbles that rattled in time with the rhythm of the dance. In piping soprano they sang a lively air which, unlike any native music I had hitherto heard, sounded distinctly European, and would scarcely have been out of place in a comic opera.

When the dance was finished the Sultani came back with me to my tent, and sitting down on his stool beside me, we gossiped until I was ready to go to bed. I had given him a gorgeous green umbrella and a most meritorious knife, promising him further presents should success attend me in the chase. He, in addition to the customary cocoanuts, had presented me with some chickens and a large supply of a carrot-shaped root called mihogo; by no means a bad substitute for potatoes, and eaten either raw or cooked; having in the former state a slight chestnut flavor.

The first day's hunting was a blank, for although we climbed hill after hill and searched the country with my spy-glasses, we saw nothing but some kongoni (hartebeeste), and I had no intention

The Death Dance of the Wa Nyika children in memory of the chieftain's little son

of risking disturbing the country by shooting at them, much as the men would have liked the meat. It was the rainy season, and we were continually getting drenched by showers, but between times the sun would appear and in an incredibly short time we would be dry again. The Sultani had given me two guides, sturdy, cheerful fellows with no idea of hunting, but knowing the country well, which was all we wanted. We loaded them down with cocoanuts, for in the middle of the day when one was feeling tired and hot it was most refreshing to cut a hole in a cocoanut and drink the milk, eating the meat afterward.

The following day we made a very early start, leaving camp amid a veritable tropical downpour. For half an hour we threaded our way through the semi-cultivated native shambas; the rain soon stopped, the sun rose, and we followed an over-grown trail through a jungle of glistening leaves. Climbing a large hill, we sat down among some rocks to reconnoitre. Just as I was lighting my pipe I saw Juma Yohari, one of my gun-bearers, motioning excitedly. I crept over to him and he pointed out, three-quarters of a mile away, a small band of sable crossing a lit-tle open space between two thickets. The country was difficult to hunt, for it was so furrowed with valleys, down the most of which there ran streams, that there was very little level land, and that little was in the main bush country—the Bara, as the natives called it. There were, however, occasional open stretches, but during the rainy season, as at present, the grass was so high everywhere that it was difficult to find game. We held a hurried consultation, Juma, Kasitura—my other gun-bearer—and myself; after a short disagreement we decided upon the course, and set out as fast as we safely could toward the point agreed on. It was exhausting work: through ravines, up hills, all amid a tan-gle of vines and thorns; and once among the valleys it was hard to know just where we were. When we reached what we felt was the spot we had aimed at, we could find no trace of our quarry, though we searched stealthily in all directions. I led the way toward a cluster of tall palms that were surrounded by dense undergrowth. A slight wind rose, and as I entered the thicket with every nerve tense, I heard a loud and most disconcerting crackle that caused me to jump back on to Yohari, who was close behind me. He grinned and pointed to some great dead palm-leaves pendant along the trunk of one of the trees that the wind had set in motion. The next instant I caught sight of a pair of horns moving through the brush. On making out the general outline of the body, I fired. Another antelope that I had not seen made off, and taking it for a female I again fired, bringing it down with a most lucky shot. I had hoped to collect male, female, and young for the museum, so I was overjoyed, believing that I had on the second day's hunting managed to get the two adults. Yohari and Kasitura thought the same, but when we reached our quarry we found them to be both males; the latter a young one, and the former, although full grown in body, by no means the tawny black color of an old bull. We set to work on the skins, and soon had them off. Juma took one of the Shenzies[1] and went back to camp with the skins, while Kasitura and I went on with the other. We returned to camp by moonlight that night without having seen any more game. The porters had gone out and brought in the meat and there was a grand feast in progress.

After some antelope-steak and a couple of cups of tea I tumbled into bed and was soon sound asleep. The next thing I knew I was wide awake, feeling as if there were fourscore pincers at work on me. Bounding out of bed, I ran for the camp-fire, which was still flickering. I was covered with ants. They had apparently attacked the boys sleeping near me at about the same time, for the camp was in an uproar and there was a hurrying of black figures, and a torrent of angry Swahili imprecations. There was nothing for it but to beat an ignominious retreat, and we fled in confusion. Once out of reach of reinforcements we soon ridded ourselves of such of our adversaries as were still on us. Fortunately for us the assault had taken place not long before dawn, and we returned to camp safely by daylight.

That day we moved camp to the top of a neighboring hill, about a mile from the village. I spent the morning working over the skins which I had only roughly salted the night before; but in the afternoon we sallied forth again to the hunt.

We went through several unsuccessful days before I again came up with sable. Several times we had met with fresh tracks, and in each case Kasitura, who was a strapping Basoga from a tribe far inland and an excellent tracker, took up the trail and did admirable work. The country was invariably so dense and the game so wary that in spite of Kasitura's remarkable tracking, only on two occasions did we sight the quarry, and each time it was only a fleeting glimpse as they crashed off. I could have had a shot, but I was anxious not to kill anything more save a full-grown female or an old master bull; and it was impossible to determine either sex or age.

On what was to be our last day's hunting we made a particularly early start and pushed on and on through the wild bushland, stopping occasionally to spy round from some vantage-point. We would swelter up a hill, down into the next valley among the lovely tall trees that lined the brook, cross the cool, rock-strewn stream, and on again. The sable fed in the open only in the very early morning till about nine o'clock, then they would retreat into the thickets and doze until four or five in the afternoon, when they would again come out to feed. During the intervening time our only chance was to run across them by luck, or find fresh tracks to follow. On that particular day we climbed a high hill about noon to take a look round and have a couple of hours' siesta. I found a shady tree and sat down with my back against the trunk. Ten miles or so away sparkled and shimmered the Indian Ocean. On all sides stretched the wonderful bushland, here and there in the distance broken by little patches of half-cultivated land. There had been a rain-storm in the morning, but now the sun was shining undimmed. Taking from my hunting-coat pocket Borrow's *Wild Wales*, I was soon climbing far-distant Snowdon with Lavengro, and was only brought back to realities by Juma, who came up to discuss the afternoon's campaign. We had scarcely begun when one of the Shenzies, whom I had sent to watch from a neighboring hill, came up in great excitement to say that he had found a large sable bull. We hurried along after him, and presently he pointed to a thicket ahead of us. Leaving the rest behind, Juma and I proceeded cautiously toward the thicket. We found two sable cows, which Juma felt sure were all that there were in the thicket, whereas I could not help putting some faith in the Shenzi who had been very insistent about the "big bull." I was convinced at length that Juma was right, so I took aim at the better of the cows. My shooting was poor, for I only crippled her, and when I moved up close for a final shot she attempted to charge, snorting savagely, but too badly hit to cause any trouble.

We had spent some time searching for the bull, so that by the time we had the skin off, the brief African twilight was upon us. We had been hunting very hard for the last week, and were all of us somewhat fagged, but as we started toward camp I soon forgot my weariness in the magic of the night. Before the moon rose we trooped silently along, no one speaking, but all listening to the strange noises of the wilderness. We were following a rambling native trail, which wound along a deep valley beside a stream for some time before it struck out across the hills for camp. There was but little game in the country, still occasionally we would hear a buck that had winded us crashing off, or some animal splashing across the stream. In the more open country the noise of the cicadas, loud and incessant, took me back to the sound of the katydids in summer nights on Long Island. The moon rose large and round, outlining the tall ivory-nut palms. It was as if we were marching in fairyland, and with real regret I at length caught the gleam of the camp-fire through the trees.

It was after ten o'clock, when we had had something to eat, but Juma, Kasitura, and I gathered to work on the sable, and toiled until we began to nod off to sleep as we skinned.

Across the bay from Mombasa; the porters ready to shoulder loads and march

Next morning I paid my last visit to the old Sultani, rewarding him as I had promised and solemnly agreeing to come back and live with him in his country. The porters were joyful, as is always the case when they are headed for Mombasa. Each thought of the joyous time he would have spending his earnings, and they sang in unison as they swung along the trail—careless, happy children. I, too, was in the best of spirits, for my quest had been successful, and I was not returning empty-handed.

CHAPTER III

THE SHEEP OF THE DESERT

I wished to hunt the mountain-sheep of the Mexican desert, hoping to be able to get a series needed by the National Museum.

At Yuma, on the Colorado River, in the extreme southwestern corner of Arizona, I gathered my outfit. Doctor Carl Lumholtz, the explorer, had recently been travelling and hunting in that part of Mexico. In addition to much valuable help as to outfitting, he told me how to get hold of a Mexican who had been with him and whom he had found trustworthy. The postmaster, Mr. Chandler, and Mr. Verdugo, a prominent business man, had both been more than kind in helping in every possible way. Mr. Charles Utting, clerk of the District Court, sometime Rough Rider, and inveterate prospector, was to start off with me for a short holiday from judicial duties. To him the desert was an open book, and from long experience he understood all the methods and needs of desert travel. Mr. Win Proebstel, ranchman and prospector, was also to start with us. He had shot mountain-sheep all the way from Alaska to Mexico, and was a mine of first-hand information as to their habits and seasons. I had engaged two Mexicans, Cipriano Dominguez and Eustacio Casares.

On the afternoon of the 10th of August we reached Wellton, a little station on the Southern Pacific, some forty miles east of Yuma. Win and his brother, Ike Proebstel, were ready with a wagon, which the latter was to drive to a water-hole some sixteen miles south, near some mining claims of Win's. August is the hottest month in the year in that country, a time when on the desert plains of Sonora the thermometer marks 140 degrees; so we decided to take advantage of a glorious full moon and make our first march by night. We loaded as much as we could of our outfit into the wagon, so as to save our riding and pack animals. We started at nine in the evening. The moon rode high. At first the desert stretched in unbroken monotony on all sides, to the dim and far-off mountains. In a couple of hours we came to the country of the saguaro, the giant cactus. All around us, their shafts forty or fifty feet high, with occasional branches set at grotesque angles to the trunk, they rose from the level floor of the desert, ghostly in the moonlight. The air seemed cool in comparison with the heat of the day, though the ground was still warm to the touch.

Shortly before one in the morning we reached Win's water-hole — tank, in the parlance of the country — and were soon stretched out on our blankets, fast asleep.

Next day we loaded our outfit on our two pack-mules and struck out across the desert for the Tinajas Altas (High Tanks), which lay on the slopes of a distant range of mountains, about four miles from the Mexican border. For generations these tanks have been a well-known stepping-stone in crossing the desert. There are a series of them, worn out in the solid rock and extending up a cleft in the mountainside, which, in time of rain, becomes the course of a torrent. The usual camping-place is a small plateau, a couple of hundred yards from the lowest tank. This plateau lies in a gulch and is sheltered on either hand by its steep and barren sides. A few hundred feet from the entrance, on the desert and scattered about among the cactus, lie some hundred and fifty graves — the graves of men who have died of thirst; for this is a grim land, and death dogs the footsteps of those who cross it. Most of the dead men were Mexicans who had struggled across the deserts only to find the tanks dry. Each lay where he fell, until, sooner or later, some other traveller found him and scooped out for him a shallow grave, and on it laid a pile of rocks in the shape of a rude cross. Forty-six unfortunates perished here at one time of thirst. They were making their way across the deserts to the United States, and were in the last stages of exhaustion for lack of water when they reached these tanks. But a Mexican outlaw named Blanco reached the tanks ahead of them and bailed out the water, after carefully laying in a store for himself not far away. By this cache he waited until he felt sure that his victims were dead; he then returned to the tanks, gathered the possessions of the dead, and safely made his escape.

A couple of months previously a band of insurrectos had been camped by these tanks, and two newly made graves marked their contribution. The men had been killed in a brawl.

Utting told us of an adventure that took place here, a few years ago, which very nearly had a tragic termination. It was in the winter season and there was an American camped at the tanks, when two Mexicans came there on their way to the Tule tanks, twenty-five miles away, near which they intended to do some prospecting. Forty-eight hours after they had left, one of them turned up riding their pack-mule and in a bad way for water. He said that they had found the Tule tanks dry, but had resolved to have one day's prospecting anyway; they had separated, but agreed at what time they were to meet. Although he waited for a long while after the agreed time, his companion never appeared, and he was forced to start back alone.

Twenty-four hours after the return of this Mexican, the American was awakened in the night by hearing strange sounds in the bed of the arroyo. When he went down to investigate them he found the lost Mexican; he was in a fearful condition, totally out of his head, and was vainly struggling to crawl up the bank of the arroyo, in order to make the last hundred yards across the plateau to the water-hole. He would never have reached it alone. By careful treatment the American brought him round and then listened to his story. He had lost himself when he went off prospecting, and when he finally got his bearings he was already in a very bad way for water. Those dwelling in cool, well-watered regions can hardly make themselves realize what thirst means in that burning desert. He knew that although there was no water in the Tule wells, there was some damp mud in the bottom, and he said that all he wished to do was to reach the wells and cool himself off in the mud before he died. A short distance from the tanks the trail he was following divided, one branch leading to the Tule wells and the other back to the Tinajas Altas, twenty-five miles away. The Mexican was so crazed that he took the wrong branch, and before he realized his mistake he had gone some way past Tule; he then decided that it was the hand of providence that had led him past, and that he must try to make Tinajas Altas; a feat which he would have just missed accomplishing but for the American encamped there.

The morning after we reached the tanks, the Tinah'alta, as they are called colloquially, Win and I were up and off for the hunting-grounds by half past three; by sun-up we were across the border, and hunted along the foot of the mountains, climbing across the out-jutting ridges. At about nine we reached the top of a ridge and began looking around. Win called to me that he saw some sheep. We didn't manage things very skilfully, and the sheep took fright, but as they stopped I shot at a fine ram. Win's rifle echoing my shot. We neither of us scored a hit, and missed several running shots. This missing was mere bad luck on Win's part, for he was a crack shot, and later on that day, when we were not together, he shot a ram, only part of which was visible, at a distance of three hundred and fifty yards. As the sun grew hotter we hunted farther up on the mountains, but we saw no more sheep, and returned to camp with Utting, who met us at a ravine near the border.

After we got back to camp, Win and I filled some canteens, threw our blankets on one of the pack-mules, took Dominguez, and rode back over the border to camp in the dry bed of an arroyo near where we had been hunting in the morning. We sent back the animals, arranging with Dominguez to return with them the following day. Next morning at a little after three we rolled out of our blankets, built a little fire of mesquite wood, and after a steaming cup of coffee and some cold frying-pan bread we shouldered our rifles and set out. At the end of several hours' steady walking I got a chance at a fair ram and missed. I sat down and took out my field-glasses to try to see where he went; and I soon picked up three sheep standing on a great boulder, near the foot of a mountain of the same range that we were on. They were watching us and were all ewes, but I wanted one for the museum. So I waited till they lost interest in us, got down from the rock, and disappeared from our sight. I then left Win and started toward the boulder; after some rather careful stalking I got one of them at about two hundred yards by some fairly creditable shooting. The side of the mountain range along which we were hunting was cut by numerous deep gullies from two to three hundred yards across. After I had dressed the ewe I thought I would go a little way farther, on the chance of coming upon the ram I had missed; for he had disappeared in that direction. When I had crossed three or four ridges I sat down to look around. It was about half past nine, the heat was burning, and I knew the sheep would soon be going up the mountains to seek the shelter of the caves in which they spend the noonday hours. Suddenly I realized that there were some sheep on the side of the next ridge standing quietly watching me. There were four bunches, scattered among the rocks; three were of ewes and young, and there was one bunch of rams; in all there were sixteen sheep. I picked out the best ram, and, estimating the distance at two hundred and fifty yards, I fired, hitting, but too low. I failed to score in the running shooting, but when he was out of sight I hurried over and picked up the trail; he was bleeding freely, and it was not difficult to follow him. He went half a mile or so and then lay down in a rock cave; but he was up and off before I could labor into sight, and made a most surprising descent down the side of a steep ravine. When I caught sight of him again he was half-way up the opposite wall of the ravine though only about a hundred yards distant; he was standing behind a large rock with only his quarters visible, but one more shot brought matters to a finish. The heat was very great, so I

A desert camp in old Mexico

started right to work to get the skin off. A great swarm of bees gathered to the feast. They were villainous-looking, and at first they gave me many qualms, but we got used to each other and I soon paid no attention to them, merely brushing them off any part that I wanted to skin. I was only once stung, and that was when a bee got inside my clothing and I inadvertently squeezed it. Before I had finished the skinning I heard a shot from Win; I replied, and a little while afterward he came along. I shall not soon forget packing the skin, with the head and the leg-bones still in it, down that mountainside. In addition to being very heavy, it made an unwieldy bundle, as I had no rope with which to tie it up. I held the head balanced on one shoulder, with a horn hooked round my neck; the legs I bunched together as best I could, but they were continually coming loose and causing endless trouble. After I reached the bottom, I left Win with the sheep and struck off for our night's camping-place. It was after eleven and the very hottest part of the day. I had to be careful not to touch any of the metal part of my gun; indeed, the wooden stock was unpleasantly hot, and I was exceedingly glad that there was to be water waiting for me at camp.

I got Dominguez and the horses and brought in the sheep, which took several hours. That afternoon we were back at Tinah'alta, with a long evening's work ahead of me skinning out the heads and feet by starlight. Utting, who was always ready to do anything at any time, and did everything well, turned to with a will and took the ewe off my hands.

The next day I was hard at work on the skins. One of the tanks, about four hundred yards from camp, was a great favorite with the sheep, and more than once during our stay the men in camp saw sheep come down to drink at it. This had generally happened when I was off hunting; but on the morning when I was busy with the skins two rams came down to drink. It was an hour before noon; for at this place the sheep finished feeding before they drank. The wind was blowing directly up the gulch to them, but although they stopped several times to stare at the camp, they eventually came to the water-hole and drank. Of course we didn't disturb these sheep, for not only were they in the United States, but they were drinking at a water-hole in a desert country; and a man who has travelled the deserts, and is any sort of a sportsman, would not shoot game at a water-hole unless he were in straits for food.

I had been hunting on the extreme end of the Gila Range and near a range called El Viejo Hombre (The Old Man). After I shot my ram, in the confusion that followed, two of the young rams broke back, came down the mountain, passing quite close to Win, and crossed the plain to the Viejo Hombre Range, some mile and a half away. The bands of sheep out of which I shot my specimens had been feeding chiefly on the twigs of a small symmetrical bush, called by the Mexicans El Yervo del Baso, the same, I believe, that Professor Hornaday in his *Camp-Fires on Desert and Lava* calls the white Brittle bush. They had also been eating such galleta-grass as they could find; it was on this grass that we depended for food for our horses and mules. Apparently the sheep of these bands had not been going to the water-hole; there were numerous places where they had been breaking down cactus and eating the pulp. In this country Win said that the rams and the ewes began to run together in October, and that in February the young were born. When the rams left the ewes, they took with them the yearling rams, and they didn't join the ewes again until the next October.

On the following day I left Utting and Proebstel and took the trail to the Tule tank. The two Mexicans were with me and we had two horses and three mules. We were travelling very light, for we were bound for a country where water-holes were not only few and far between but most uncertain. My personal baggage consisted of my washing kit, an extra pair of shoes, a change of socks, and a couple of books. Besides our bedding we had some coffee, tea, sugar, rice, flour (with a little bacon to take the place of lard in making bread), and a good supply of frijoles, or Mexican beans. It was on these last that we really lived. As soon as we got to a camp we always put some frijoles in a kettle and started a little fire to boil them. If we were to be there for a couple of days we put in enough beans to last us the whole time, and then all that was necessary in getting a meal ready was to warm up the beans.

It was between four and five in the afternoon when we left Tinah'alta, and though the moon did not rise until late, the stars were bright and the trail was clear. The desert we were riding through was covered with mesquite and creosote and innumerable choya cactus; there were also two kinds of prickly-pear cactus, and ocatillas were plentiful. The last are curious plants; they are formed somewhat on the principle of an umbrella, with a very short central stem from which sometimes as many as twenty spokes radiate umbrella-wise. These spokes are generally about six feet long and are covered with thorns which are partially concealed by tiny leaves. The flower of the ocatilla is scarlet, and although most of them had stopped flowering by August, there were a few still in bloom. After about six hours' silent riding we reached Tule. The word means a marsh, but, needless to say, all that we found was a rock-basin with a fair supply of water and a very generous supply of tadpoles and water-lice.

Next morning when we came to get breakfast ready we found we had lost, through a hole in a pack-sack, all of our eating utensils except a knife and two spoons; but we were thankful at having got off so easily. By three in the afternoon we were ready for what was to be our hardest march. We wished to get into the Pinacate country; and our next water was to be the Papago tank, which Casares said was about forty-five miles south of us. He said that in this tank we were always sure to find water.

For the first fifteen miles our route lay over the Camino del Diablo, a trail running through the Tule desert—and it has proved indeed a "road of the devil" for many an unfortunate. Then we left the trail, the sun sank, twilight passed, and in spite of the brilliancy of the stars, the going became difficult. In many places where the ground was free from boulders the kangaroo-rats had made a network of tunnels, and into these our animals fell, often sinking shoulder-deep. Casares was leading, riding a hardy little white mule. While he rode he rolled cigarette after cigarette, and as he bent forward in his saddle to light them, for a moment his face would be brought into relief by the burning match and a trail of sparks would light up the succeeding darkness. Once his mule shied violently, and we heard the angry rattling of a side-winder, a sound which once heard is never forgotten.

At about eight o'clock, what with rocks and kangaroo-rat burrows, the going became so bad that we decided to offsaddle and wait till the moon should rise. We stretched out with our heads on our saddles and dozed until about midnight, when it was time to start on again. Soon the desert changed and we were free of the hills among which we had been travelling, and were riding over endless rolling dunes of white sand. As dawn broke, the twin peaks of Pinacate appeared ahead of us, and the sand gave place to a waste of red and black lava, broken by steep arroyos. We had been hearing coyotes during the night, and now a couple jumped up from some rocks, a hundred yards away, and made off amongst the lava.

By eight o'clock the sun was fiercely hot, but we were in among the foot-hills of Pinacate. I asked Casares where the tanks were, and he seemed rather vague, but said they were beyond the next hills. They were not; but several times more he felt sure they were "just around the next hill." I realized that we were lost and resolved to give him one more try, and then if I found that he was totally at sea as to the whereabouts of the tank, I intended to find some shelter for the heat of the day, and, when it got cooler, to throw the packs off our animals and strike back to Tule. It is difficult to realize how quickly that fierce sun dries up man and beast. I doubt if in that country a really good walker could have covered ten miles in the noonday heat without water and without stopping. We could have made Tule all right, but the return trip would have been a very unpleasant one, and we would probably have lost some of our animals.

However, just before we reached Casares's last location of the Papago tanks, we came upon an unknown water-hole, in the bed of an arroyo. The rains there are very local, and although the rest

Casares on his white mule

of the country was as dry as tinder, some fairly recent downpour had filled up this little rocky basin. There were two trees near it, a mesquite and a palo verde, and though neither would fit exactly into the category of shade-trees, we were most grateful to them for being there at all. The palo verde is very deceptive. When seen from a distance, its greenness gives it a false air of being a lovely, restful screen from the sun, but when one tries to avail oneself of its shade, the fallacy is soon evident. It is only when there is some parasitical mistletoe growing on it that the palo verde offers any real shade. The horses were very thirsty, and it was a revelation to see how they lowered the water in the pool.

Dominguez was only about thirty years old, but he seemed jaded and tired, whereas Casares, who was white-haired, and must have been at least sixty, was as fresh as ever. Two days later, when I was off hunting on the mountains, Casares succeeded in finding the Papago tanks; they were about fifteen miles to our northwest, and were as dry as a bone! I later learned that a Mexican had come through this country some three weeks before we were in there. He had a number of pack-animals. When he found the Papago dry, he struck on for the next water, and succeeded in making it only after abandoning his packs and losing most of his horses.

We sat under our two trees during the heat of the day; but shortly after four I took my rifle and my canteen and went off to look for sheep, leaving the two Mexicans in camp. Although I saw no rams, I found plenty of sign and got a good idea of the lay of the land.

The next four or five days I spent hunting from this camp. I was very anxious to get some antelope, and I spent three or four days in a fruitless search for them. It was, I believe, unusually dry, even for that country, and the antelope had migrated to better feeding-grounds. Aside from a herd of nine, which I saw from a long way off but failed to come up with, not only did I not see any antelope, but I did not even find any fresh tracks. There were many very old tracks, and I have no doubt that, at certain times of the year, there are great numbers of antelope in the country over which I was hunting.

The long rides, however, were full of interest. I took the Mexicans on alternate days, and we always left camp before daylight. As the hours wore on, the sun would grow hotter and hotter. In the middle of the day there was generally a breeze blowing across the lava-beds, and that breeze was like the blast from a furnace. There are few whom the desert, at sunset and sunrise, fails to fascinate; but only those who have the love of the wastes born in them feel the magic of their appeal under the scorching noonday sun. Reptile life was abundant; lizards scuttled away in every direction; there were some rather large ones that held their tails up at an oblique angle above the ground as they ran, which gave them a ludicrous appearance. A species of toad whose back was speckled with red was rather common. Jack-rabbits and cottontails were fairly numerous, and among the birds Gambel's quail and the whitewings, or sonora pigeons, were most in evidence. I came upon one of these later on her nest in a palo-verde-tree; the eggs were about the size of a robin's and were white, and the nest was made chiefly of galleta-grass. The whitewings are very fond of the fruit of the saguaro; this fruit is of a reddish-orange color when ripe, and the birds peck a hole in it and eat the scarlet pulp within. It is delicious, and the Indians collect it and dry it; the season was over when I was in the country, but there was some late fruit on a few of the trees. When I was back in camp at sunset it was pleasant to hear the pigeons trilling as they flew down to the pool to drink.

One day we returned to the camp at about two. I was rather hot and tired, so I made a cup of tea and sat under the trees and smoked my pipe until almost four. Then I picked up my rifle and went out by myself to look for sheep. I climbed to the top of a great crater hill and sat down to look around with my field-glasses. Hearing a stone move behind, I turned very slowly around. About a hundred and fifty yards off, on the rim of the crater, stood six sheep, two of them fine rams. Very slowly I put down the field-glasses and raised my rifle, and I killed the finer of the rams. It was getting dark, so, without bestowing more than a passing look upon him, I struck off for camp at a round pace. Now the Mexicans, although good enough in the saddle, were no walkers, and so Dominguez saddled a horse, put a pack-saddle on a mule, and followed me back to where the sheep lay. We left the animals at the foot of the hill, and although it was not a particularly hard climb up to the sheep, the Mexican was blown and weary by the time we reached it. The ram was a good one. His horns measured sixteen and three-fourths inches around the base and were thirty-five inches long, so they were larger in circumference though shorter than my first specimen. He was very thin, however, and his hair was falling out, so that one could pull it out in handfuls. All the sheep that I saw in this country seemed thin and in poor shape, while those near Tinah'alta were in very fair condition. The extreme dryness and scarcity of grass doubtless in part accounted for this, although the country in which I got my first two sheep was in no sense green. Making our way back to camp through the lava-fields and across the numerous gullies was a difficult task. The horses got along much better than I should have supposed; indeed, they didn't seem to find as much difficulty as I did. Dominguez muttered that if the road past Tule was the Camino del Diablo, this certainly was the Camino del Infierno! When we reached camp my clothes were as wet as if I had been in swimming. I set right to work on the headskin, but it was eleven o'clock before I had finished it; that meant but four hours' sleep for me, and I felt somewhat melancholy about it. Indeed, on this trip, the thing that I chiefly felt was the need of sleep, for it was always necessary to make a very early start, and it was generally after sunset before I got back to camp.

The Mexicans spoke about as much English as I spoke Spanish, which was very little, and as they showed no signs of learning, I set to work to learn some Spanish. At first our conversation was very limited, but I soon got so that I could understand them pretty well. We occasionally tried to tell each other stories but became so confused that we would have to call it off. Dominguez had one English expression which he would pronounce with great pride and emphasis on all appropriate or inappropriate occasions; it was

"You betcher!" Once he and I had some discussion as to what day it was and I appealed to Casares. "Ah, quien sabe, quien sabe?" (who knows, who knows?) was his reply; he said that he never knew what day it was and got on very comfortably without knowing—a point of view which gave one quite a restful feeling. They christened our water-hole Tinaja del Bévora, which means the tank of the rattlesnake. They so named it because of the advent in camp one night of a rattler. It escaped and got in a small lava-cave, from out of which the men tried long and unsuccessfully to smoke it.

At the place where we were camped our arroyo had tunnelled its way along the side of a hill; so that, from its bed, one bank was about ten feet high and the other nearer fifty. In the rocky wall of this latter side there were many caves. One, in particular, would have furnished good sleeping quarters for wet weather. It was about twenty-five feet long and fifteen feet deep, and it varied in height from four to six feet. The signs showed that for generations it had been a favorite abode of sheep; coyotes had also lived in it, and in the back there was a big pack-rat's nest. Pieces of the bisnaga cactus, with long, cruel spikes, formed a prominent part of the nest.

After I had hunted for antelope in every direction from camp, and within as large a radius as I could manage, I was forced to admit the hopelessness of the task. The water-supply was getting low, but I determined to put in another good long day with the sheep before turning back. Accordingly, early one morning, I left the two Mexicans in camp to rest and set off for the mountains on foot. I headed for the main peak of Pinacate. It was not long before I got in among the foot-hills. I kept down along the ravines, for it was very early, and as a rule the sheep didn't begin to go up the hills from their night's feeding until nine or ten o'clock; at this place, also, they almost always spent the noon hours in caves. There were many little chipmunks running along with their tails arched forward over their backs, which gave them rather a comical look. At length I saw a sheep; he was well up the side of a large hill, an old crater, as were many of these mountains. I made off

Making fast the sheep's head

after him and found there were steep ravines to be reckoned with before I even reached the base of the hill. The sides of the crater were covered with choyas, and the footing on the loose lava was so uncertain that I said to myself, "I wonder how long it will be before you fall into one of these choyas," and only a few minutes later I was gingerly picking choya burrs off my arms, which had come off worst in the fall. The points of the spikes are barbed and are by no means easy to pull out. I stopped many times to wait for my courage to rise sufficiently to start to work again, and by the time I had got myself free I was so angry that I felt like devoting the rest of my day to waging a war of retaliation upon the cactus. The pain from the places from which I had pulled out the spikes lasted for about half an hour after I was free of them, and later, at Yuma, I had to have some of the spines that I had broken off in my flesh cut out.

An hour or so later I came across a very fine bisnaga, or "niggerhead," cactus. I was feeling very thirsty, and, wishing to save my canteen as long as possible, I decided to cut the bisnaga open and eat some of its pulp, for this cactus always contains a good supply of sweetish water. As I was busy trying to remove the long spikes, I heard a rock fall, and looking round saw a sheep walking along the opposite side of the gully, and not more than four hundred yards away. He was travelling slowly and had not seen me, so I hastily made for a little ridge toward which he was heading. I reached some rocks near the top of the ridge in safety and crouched behind them. I soon saw that he was only a two-year-old, and when he was two hundred yards off I stood up to have a good look at him. When he saw me, instead of immediately making off, he stood and gazed at me. I slowly sat down and his curiosity quite overcame him. He proceeded to stalk me in a most scientific manner, taking due advantage of choyas and rocks; and cautiously poking his head out from behind them to stare at me. He finally got to within fifty feet of me, but suddenly, and for no apparent reason, he took fright and made off. He did not go far, and, from a distance of perhaps five hundred yards, watched me as I resumed operations on the cactus.

Not long after this, as I was standing on the top of a hill, I made out two sheep, half hidden in a draw. There was a great difference in the size of their horns, and, in the hasty glance I got of them, one seemed to me to be big enough to warrant shooting. I did not discover my mistake until I had brought down my game. He was but a two-year-old, and, although I should have been glad of a good specimen for the museum, his hide was in such poor condition that it was quite useless. However, I took his head and some meat and headed back for camp. My camera, water-bottle, and field-glasses were already slung over my shoulder, and the three hours' tramp back to camp, in the very hottest part of the day, was tiring; and I didn't feel safe in finishing my canteen until I could see camp.

The next day we collected as much galleta-grass as we could for the horses, and, having watered them well, an operation which practically finished our pool, we set out for Tule at a little after three. As soon as the Mexicans got a little saddle-stiff they would stand up in one stirrup, crooking the other knee over the saddle, and keeping the free heel busy at the horses' ribs. The result was twofold: the first and most obvious being a sore back for the horses, and the second being that the horses became so accustomed to a continual tattoo to encourage them to improve their pace, that, with a rider unaccustomed to that method, they lagged most annoyingly. The ride back to Tule was as uneventful as it was lovely.

On the next day's march, from Tule toward Win's tank, I saw the only Gila monster—the sluggish, poisonous lizard of the southwestern deserts—that I came across throughout the trip. He was crossing the trail in leisurely fashion and darted his tongue out angrily as I stopped to admire him. Utting told me of an interesting encounter he once saw between a Gila monster and a rattlesnake. He put the two in a large box; they were in opposite corners, but presently the Gila monster started slowly and sedately toward the rattler's side of the box. He paid absolutely no attention to the snake, who coiled himself up and rattled angrily. When the lizard got near enough, the rattler struck out two or three times, each time burying his fangs in the Gila monster's body; the latter showed not the slightest concern, and, though Utting waited expectantly for him to die, he apparently suffered no ill effects whatever from the encounter. He showed neither anger nor pain; he simply did not worry himself about the rattler at all.

We reached Wellton at about nine in the evening of the second day from Pinacate. We had eaten all our food, and our pack-animals were practically without loads; so we had made ninety miles in about fifty-five hours. Dominguez had suffered from the heat on the way back, and at Win's tank, which was inaccessible to the horses, I had been obliged myself to pack all the water out to the animals. At Wellton I parted company with the Mexicans, with the regret one always feels at leaving the comrades of a hunting trip that has proved both interesting and successful.

CHAPTER IV

AFTER MOOSE IN NEW BRUNSWICK

It was early in September when the four of us—Clarke, Jamieson, Thompson, and myself—landed at Bathurst, on Chaleur Bay, and took the little railroad which runs twenty miles up the Nepisiquit River to some iron-mines. From that point we expected to pole up the river about forty miles farther and then begin our hunting.

For the four hunters—"sports" was what the guides called us— there were six guides. Three of them bore the name Venneau; there were Bill Grey and his son Willie, and the sixth was Wirre (pronounced Warry) Chamberlain. Among themselves the guides spoke French—or a corruption of French—which was hard to understand and which has come down from generation to generation without ever getting into written form. A fine-looking six they were,—straight,—with the Indian showing in their faces.

At the end of the third day of poling—a lazy time for the "sports," but three days of marvellously skilful work for the guides —our heavily laden canoes were brought up to the main camp. From here we expected to start our hunting expeditions, each taking a guide, blankets, and food, and striking off for the more isolated cabins in the woods. My purpose was to collect specimens for the National Museum at Washington. I wanted moose, caribou, and beaver—a male and female of each species. Whole skins and leg-bones were to be brought out.

A hard rain woke us, and the prospects were far from cheerful as we packed and prepared to separate. Bill Grey was to be my guide, and the "Popple Cabin," three miles away, was to be our shelter. Our tramp through the wet woods—pine, hemlock, birch, and poplar—ended at the little double lean-to shelter. After we had started a fire and spread our blankets to dry we set off in search of game.

We climbed out of the valley in which we were camped and up to the top of a hill from which we could get a good view of some small barren stretches that lay around us. It was the blueberry season, and these barrens were covered with bushes, all heavily laden. We moved around from hill to hill in search of game, but saw only three deer. We'd have shot one of them for meat, but didn't care to run the chance of frightening away any moose or caribou. The last hill we climbed overlooked a small pond which lay beside a pine forest on the edge of a barren strip. Bill intended to spend a good part of each day watching this pond, and it was to a small hill overlooking it that we made our way early next morning.

Before we had been watching many minutes, a cow moose with a calf appeared at the edge of the woods. She hesitated for several minutes, listening intently and watching sharply, and then stepped out across the barren on her way to the pond. Before she had gone far, the path she was following cut the trail we had made on our way to the lookout hill. She stopped immediately and began to sniff at our tracks, the calf following her example; a few seconds were enough to convince her, but for some reason, perhaps to make doubly sure, she turned and for some minutes followed along our trail with her nose close to the ground. Then she swung round and struck off into the woods at a great slashing moose trot.

Not long after she had disappeared, we got a fleeting glimpse of two caribou cows; they lacked the impressive ungainliness of the moose, and in the distance might easily have been mistaken for deer.

It was a very cold morning, and throughout the day it snowed and sleeted at intervals. We spent the time wandering from hill to hill.

For the next week we hunted industriously in every direction from the Popple Cabin. In the morning and the evening we shifted from hill to hill; the middle of the day we hunted along the numerous brooks that furrowed the country. With the exception of one or two days, the weather was uniformly cold and rainy; but after our first warm sunny day we welcomed rain and cold, for then, at least, we had no black flies to fight. On the two sunny days they surrounded us in swarms and made life almost unbearable; they got into our blankets and kept us from sleeping during the nights; they covered us with lumps and sores—Bill said that he had never seen them as bad.

It was lovely in the early morning to stand on some high hill and watch the mist rising lazily from the valley; it was even more lovely to watch the approach of a rain-storm. The sunlight on some distant hillside or valley would suddenly be blotted out by a sheet of rain; a few minutes later the next valley would be darkened as the storm swept toward us, and perhaps before it reached us we could see the farther valleys over which it had passed lightening again.

We managed to cover a great deal of ground during that week, and were rewarded by seeing a fair amount of game—four caribou, of which one was a bull, a bull and three cow moose, and six does and one buck deer. I had but one shot, and that was at a buck deer. We wanted meat very much, and Bill said that he didn't think one shot would disturb the moose and caribou. He was a very large buck, in prime condition; I never tasted better venison. Had our luck been a little better, I would have had a shot at a moose and a caribou; we saw the latter from some distance, and made a long and successful stalk until Wirre, on his way from the main camp with some fresh supplies, frightened our quarry away.

On these trips between camps, Wirre several times saw moose and caribou within range.

A noonday halt on the way down river, returning from the hunting country

After a week we all foregathered at the main camp. Clarke had shot a fine bear and Jamieson brought in a good moose head. They started down-river with their trophies, and Thompson and I set out for new hunting-grounds. As Bill had gone with Jamieson, I took his son Willie, a sturdy, pony-built fellow of just my age. We crossed the river and camped some two miles beyond it and about a mile from the lake we intended to hunt. We put up a lean-to, and in front of it built a great fire of old pine logs, for the nights were cold.

My blankets were warm, and it was only after a great deal of wavering hesitation that I could pluck up courage to roll out of them in the penetrating cold of early morning. On the second morning, as we made our way through dew-soaked underbrush to the lake, we came out upon a little glade, at the farther end of which stood a caribou. He sprang away as he saw us, but halted behind a bush to reconnoitre — the victim of a fatal curiosity, for it gave me my opportunity and I brought him down. Although he was large in body, he had a very poor head. I spent a busy morning preparing the skin, but in the afternoon we were again at the lake watching for moose. We spent several fruitless days there.

One afternoon a yearling bull moose appeared: he had apparently lost his mother, for he wandered aimlessly around for several hours, bewailing his fate. This watching would have been pleasant enough as a rest-cure, but since I was hunting and very anxious to get my game, it became a rather irksome affair. However, I could only follow Saint Augustine's advice, "when in Rome, fast on Saturdays," and I resigned myself to adopting Willie's plan of waiting for the game to come to us instead of pursuing my own inclination and setting out to find the game. Luckily, I had some books with me, and passed the days pleasantly enough reading Voltaire and Boileau. There was a beaver-house at one end of the lake, and between four and five the beaver would come out and swim around. I missed a shot at one. Red squirrels were very plentiful and would chatter excitedly at us from a distance of a few feet. There was one particularly persistent little chap who did everything in his power to attract attention. He would sit in the conventional squirrel attitude upon a branch, and chirp loudly, bouncing stiffly forward at each chirp, precisely as if he were an automaton.

When we decided that it was useless to hunt this lake any longer, we went back to the river to put in a few days hunting up and down it. I got back to the camp in the evening and found Thompson there. He had had no luck and intended to leave for the settlement in the morning. Accordingly, the next day he started down-stream and we went up. We hadn't been gone long before we heard what we took to be two shots, though, for all we knew, they might have been a beaver striking the water with his tail. That night, when we got back to camp, we found that, on going round a bend in the river about a mile below camp, Thompson had come upon a bull and a cow moose, and had bagged the bull.

The next morning it was raining as if it were the first storm after a long drought, and as we felt sure that no sensible moose would wander around much amid such a frozen downpour, we determined to put in a day after beaver. In one of my long tramps with Bill we had come across a large beaver-pond, and at the time Bill had remarked how easy it would be to break the dam and shoot the beaver. I had carefully noted the location of this pond, so managed successfully to pilot Willie to it, and we set to work to let the water out. This breaking the dam was not the easy matter I had imagined. It was a big pond, and the dam that was stretched across its lower end was from eight to ten feet high. To look at its solid structure and the size of the logs that formed it, it seemed inconceivable that an animal the size of a beaver could have built it. The water was above our heads, and there was a crust of ice around the edges. We had to get in and work waist-deep in the water to enlarge our break in the dam, and the very remembrance of that cold morning's work, trying to pry out logs with frozen fingers, makes me shiver. It was even worse when we had to stop work and wait and watch for the beavers to come out. They finally did, and I shot two. They were fine large specimens; the male was just two inches less than four feet and the female only one inch shorter. Shivering and frozen, we headed back for camp. My hunting costume had caused a good deal of comment among the guides; it consisted of a sleeveless cotton undershirt, a many-pocketed coat, a pair of short khaki trousers reaching to just above my knees, and then a pair of sneakers or of high boots—I used the former when I wished to walk quietly. My knees were always bare and were quite as impervious to cold as my hands, but the guides could never understand why I didn't freeze. I used to hear them solemnly discussing it in their broken French.

I had at first hoped to get my moose by fair stalking, without the help of calling, but I had long since abandoned that hope; and Willie, who was an excellent caller, had been doing his best, but with no result. We saw several cow moose, and once Willie called out a young bull, but his horns could not have had a spread of more than thirty-five inches, and he would have been quite useless as a museum specimen. Another time, when we were crawling up to a lake not far from the river, we found ourselves face to face with a two-year-old bull. He was very close to us, but as he hadn't got our wind, he was merely curious to find out what we were, for Willie kept grunting through his birch-bark horn. Once he came up to within twenty feet of us and stood gazing. Finally he got our wind and crashed off through the lakeside alders.

As a rule, moose answer a call better at night, and almost every night we could hear them calling around our camp; generally they were cows that we heard, and once Willie had a duel with a cow as to which should have a young bull that we could hear in an alder thicket, smashing the bushes with his horns. Willie finally triumphed, and the bull headed toward us with a most disconcerting rush; next morning we found his tracks at the edge of the clearing not more than twenty yards from where we had been standing; at that point the camp smoke and smells had proved more convincing than Willie's calling-horn.

Late one afternoon I had a good opportunity to watch some beaver at work. We had crawled cautiously up to a small lake in the vain hope of finding a moose, when we came upon some beaver close to the shore. Their house was twenty or thirty yards away, and they were bringing out a supply of wood, chiefly poplar, for winter food. To and fro they swam, pushing the wood in front of them. Occasionally one would feel hungry, and then he would stop and start eating the bark from the log he was pushing. It made me shiver to watch them lying lazily in that icy water.

I had already stayed longer than I intended, and the day was rapidly approaching when I should have to start down-river. Even the cheerful Willie was getting discouraged, and instead of accounts of the miraculous bags hunters made at the end of their trips, I began to be told of people who were unfortunate enough to go out without anything. I made up my mind to put in the last few days hunting from the Popple Cabin, so one rainy noon, after a morning's hunt along the river, we shouldered our packs and tramped off to the little cabin from which Bill and I had hunted. Wirre was with us, and we left him to dry out the cabin while we went off to try a late afternoon's hunt. As we were climbing the hill from which Bill and I used to watch the little pond, Willie caught sight of a moose on the side of a hill a mile away. One look through our field-glasses convinced us it was a good bull. A deep wooded valley intervened, and down into it we started at headlong speed, and up the other side we panted. As we neared where we believed the moose to be, I slowed down in order to get my wind in case I had to do some quick shooting. I soon picked up the moose and managed to signal Willie to stop. The moose was walking along at the edge of the woods somewhat over two hundred yards to our left. The wind was favorable, so I decided to try to get nearer before shooting. It was a mistake, for which I came close to paying dearly; suddenly, and without any warning, the great animal swung into the woods and disappeared before I could get ready to shoot.

Willie had his birch-bark horn with him and he tried calling, but instead of coming toward us, we could hear the moose moving off in the other direction. The woods were dense, and all chance seemed to have gone. With a really good tracker, such as are to be

Bringing out the trophies of the hunt

found among some of the African tribes, the task would have been quite simple, but neither Willie nor I was good enough. We had given up hope when we heard the moose grunt on the hillside above us. Hurrying toward the sound, we soon came into more open country. I saw him in a little glade to our right; he looked most impressive as he stood there, nearly nineteen hands at the withers, shaking his antlers and staring at us; I dropped to my knee and shot, and that was the first that Willie knew of our quarry's presence. He didn't go far after my first shot, but several more were necessary before he fell. We hurried up to examine him; he was not yet dead, and when we were half a dozen yards away, he staggered to his feet and started for us, but he fell before he could reach us. Had I shot him the first day I might have had some compunction at having put an end to such a huge, handsome animal, but as it was I had no such feelings. We had hunted long and hard, and luck had been consistently against us.

Our chase had led us back in a quartering direction toward camp, which was now not more than a mile away; so Willie went to get Wirre, while I set to work to take the measurements and start on the skinning. Taking off a whole moose hide is no light task, and it was well after dark before we got it off. We estimated the weight of the green hide as well over a hundred and fifty pounds, but probably less than two hundred. We bundled it up as well as we could in some pack-straps, and as I seemed best suited to the task, I fastened it on my back.

The sun had gone down, and that mile back to camp, crawling over dead falls and tripping on stones, was one of the longest I have ever walked. The final descent down the almost perpendicular hillside was the worst. When I fell, the skin was so heavy and such a clumsy affair that I couldn't get up alone unless I could find a tree to help me; but generally Willie would start me off again. When I reached the cabin, in spite of the cold night-air, my clothes were as wet as if I had been in swimming. After they had taken the skin off my shoulders, I felt as if I had nothing to hold me down to earth, and might at any moment go soaring into the air.

Next morning I packed the skin down to the main camp, about three miles, but I found it a much easier task in the daylight. After working for a while on the skin, I set off to look for a cow moose, but, as is always the case, where they had abounded before, there was none to be found now that we wanted one.

The next day we spent tramping over the barren hillsides after caribou. Willie caught a glimpse of one, but it disappeared into a pine forest before we could come up with it. On the way back to camp I shot a deer for meat on our way down the river.

I had determined to have one more try for a cow moose, and next morning was just going off to hunt some lakes when we caught sight of an old cow standing on the opposite bank of the river about half a mile above us. We crossed and hurried up along the bank, but when we reached the bog where she had been standing she had disappeared. There was a lake not far from the river-bank, and we thought that she might have gone to it, for we felt sure we had not frightened her. As we reached the lake we saw her standing at the edge of the woods on the other side, half hidden in the trees. I fired and missed, but as she turned to make off I broke her hind quarter. After going a little distance she circled back to the lake and went out to stand in the water. We portaged a canoe from the river and took some pictures before finishing the cow. At the point where she fell the banks of the lake were so steep that we had to give up the attempt to haul the carcass out. I therefore set to work to get the skin off where the cow lay in the water. It was a slow, cold task, but finally I finished and we set off down-stream, Wirre in one canoe and Willie and myself in the other. According to custom, the moose head was laid in the bow of our canoe, with the horns curving out on either side.

We had been in the woods for almost a month, and in that time we had seen the glorious changes from summer to fall and fall to early winter, for the trees were leafless and bare. Robinson's lines kept running through my head as we sped down-stream through the frosty autumn day:

"Come away! come away! there's a frost along the marshes,
And a frozen wind that skims the shoal where it shakes the
dead black water;
There's a moan across the lowland, and a wailing through
the woodland
Of a dirge that sings to send us back to the arms of those
that love us.
There is nothing left but ashes now where the crimson
chills of autumn
Put off the summer's languor, with a touch that made us glad
For the glory that is gone from us, with a flight we cannot follow,
To the slopes of other valleys, and the sounds of other shores."

CHAPTER V

TWO BOOK-HUNTERS
IN SOUTH AMERICA

In Collaboration with Mrs. Kermit Roosevelt

THE true bibliophile will always find time to exercise his calling, no matter where he happens to be, or in what manner he is engaged in making his daily bread. In some South American cities, more particularly in Buenos Ayres, there is so little to do outside of one's office that were there more old bookstores it would be what Eugene Field would have called a bibliomaniac's paradise. To us wanderers on the face of the earth serendipity in its more direct application to book-collecting is a most satisfactory pursuit; for it requires but little capital, and in our annual flittings to "somewhere else" our purchases necessitate but the minimum of travelling space. There are two classes of bibliophiles—those to whom the financial side is of little or no consequence, and those who, like the clerk of the East India House, must count their pennies, and save, and go without other things to counterbalance an extravagance in the purchase of a coveted edition. To the former class these notes may seem overworldly in their frequent allusion to prices; but to its authors the financial side must assume its relative importance.

Among the South American republics, Brazil undeniably takes precedence from a literary standpoint. Most Brazilians, from Lauro Muller, the minister of foreign affairs, to the postmaster of the little frontier town, have at some period in their lives published, or at all events written, a volume of prose or verse. It comes to them from their natural surroundings, and by inheritance, for once you except Cervantes, the Portuguese have a greater literature than the Spaniards. There is therefore in Brazil an excellent and widely read native literature, and in almost every home there are to be found the works of such poets as Gonçalves Diaz and Castro Alves, and historians, novelists, and essayists like Taunay, Couto de Magalhãens, Alencar, and Coelho Netto. Taunay's most famous novel, *Innocencia,* a tale of life in the frontier state of Matto Grosso — "the great wilderness" — has been translated into seven languages, including the Japanese and Polish. The literature of the mother country is also generally known; Camões is read in the schools, and a quotation from the Lusiads is readily capped by a casual acquaintance in the remotest wilderness town. Portuguese poets and playwrights like Almeda Garret, Bocage, Quental and Guerra Junquera; and historians and novelists such as Herculano, Eça de Queiroz, or Castello Branco are widely read.

In Brazil, as throughout South America, French is almost universally read; cheap editions of the classics are found in most homes, and bookstores are filled with modern French writers of prose or verse — sometimes in translation, and as frequently in the original. Rio de Janeiro and São Paulo abound in old bookstores, which are to be found in fewer numbers in others of the larger towns, such as Manaos, Para, Pernambuco, Bahia, Curytiba, or Porto Alegre. In the smaller towns of the interior one runs across only new books, although occasionally those who possess the "flaire" may chance upon some battered treasure.

The line which is of most interest, and in South America presents the greatest latitude, is undoubtedly that of early voyages and discoveries. Probably it was because they were in a greater or less degree voyagers or explorers themselves that the Americans and English who came to South America seventy or eighty years ago brought with them books of exploration and travel, both contemporary and ancient. Many of these volumes, now rare in the mother country, are to be picked up for a song in the old bookstores of the New World.

The accounts of the Conquistadores and early explorers, now in the main inaccessible except in great private collections or museums, have frequently been reprinted, and if written in a foreign tongue, translated, in the country which they describe. Thus the account of Père Yveux was translated and printed in Maranhão in 1878, and this translation is now itself rare. We picked up a copy for fifty cents in a junk-store in Bahia, but in São Paulo had to pay the market price for the less rare translation of Hans Stade's captivity. Ulrich Schmidel's entertaining account of the twenty years of his life spent in the first half of the sixteenth century in what is now Argentina, Paraguay, and Brazil, has been excellently translated into Spanish by an Argentine of French descent, Lafoyne Quevedo, the head of the La Plata museum. We had never seen the book until one day at the judicial auction held by the heirs of a prominent Argentine lawyer. Books published in Buenos Ayres are as a whole abominably printed, but this was really beautiful, so we determined to get it. The books were being sold in ill-assorted lots, and this one was with three other volumes; one was an odd volume of Italian poetry, one a religious treatise, and the third a medical book. Bidding had been low, and save for standard legal books, the lots had been going at two or three dollars apiece. Our lot quickly went to five dollars. There was soon only one man bidding against us. We could not understand what he wanted, but thought that perhaps the Schmidel was worth more than we had imagined. Our blood was up and we began trying to frighten our opponent by substantial raises; at fourteen he dropped out. The dealers in common with every one else were much intrigued at the high bidding, and clearly felt that something had escaped them. The mystery was solved when our opponent hurried over to ask what we wanted for the odd volume of Italian verse—it belonged to him and he had loaned it to the defunct lawyer shortly before his death. We halved the expenses and the lot, and, as a curious sequel, later found that the medical book which had quite accidentally fallen to our share was worth between fifteen and twenty dollars.

Prices in Brazil seemed very high in comparison with those of Portugal and Spain, but low when compared with Argentina. On the west coast we found books slightly less expensive than in Brazil, where, however, the prices have remained the same as before the war, though the drop in exchange has given the foreigner the benefit of a twenty-five per cent reduction. There are a fair number of auctions, and old books are also sold through priced lists, published in the daily papers. We obtained our best results by search in the bookshops. It was in this way that we got for three dollars the first edition of Castelleux's *Voyage dans la Partie Septentrionale de l' Amerique*, in perfect condition, and for one dollar Jordan's *Guerra do Paraguay*, for which a bookseller in Buenos Ayres had asked, as a tremendous bargain, twelve dollars.

In São Paulo after much searching we found Santos Saraiva's paraphrase of the Psalms, a famous translation, quite as beautiful as our own English version. The translator was born in Lisbon. His father was a Jewish rabbi, but he entered the Catholic Church, became a priest, and went to an inland parish in southern Brazil. After some years he left the Church and settled down with a Brazilian woman in a small, out-of-the-way fazenda, where he translated the Psalms, and also composed a Greek lexicon that is regarded as a masterpiece. He later became instructor in Greek in Mackenzie College in São Paulo, confining his versatile powers to that institution until he died.

The dearth of native literature in Buenos Ayres is not surprising, for nature has done little to stimulate it, and in its fertility much to create the commercialism that reigns supreme. The country is in large part rolling prairie-land, and although there is an attraction about it in its wild state, which has called forth a gaucho literature that chiefly takes form in long and crude ballads, the magic of the prairie-land is soon destroyed by houses, factories, dump-heaps, and tin cans. At first sight it would appear hopeless ground for a bibliophile, but with time and patience we found a fair number of old bookstores; and there rarely passes a week without a book auction, or at any rate an auction where some books are put up.

Among the pleasantest memories of our life in Buenos Ayres are those of motoring in to a sale from our house in Belgrano, along the famous Avenida Alvear, on starlit nights, with the Southern Cross high and brilliant. Occasionally when the books we were interested in were far between, we would slip out of the smoke-laden room for a cup of unrivalled coffee at the Café Paulista, or to watch Charlie Chaplin as "Carlitos" amuse the Argentine public.

The great percentage of the books one sees at auctions or in bookstores are strictly utilitarian; generally either on law or medicine. In the old bookstores there are, as in Boston, rows of religious books, on which the dust lies undisturbed. In Argentine literature there are two or three famous novels; most famous of these is probably Marmol's *Amalia*, a bloodthirsty and badly written story of the reign of Rosas—the gaucho Nero. Bunge's *Novela de la Sangre* is an excellently given but equally lurid account of the same period. *La Gloria de Don Ramiro*, by Rodriguez Larreta, is a well-written tale of the days of Philip the Second. The author, the present Argentine minister in Paris, spent some two years in Spain studying the local setting of his romance. Most Argentines, if they have not read these novels, at least know the general plots and the more important characters. The literature of the mother country is little read and as a rule looked down upon by the Argentines, who are more apt to read French or even English. *La Nacion*, which is one of the two great morning papers, and owned by a son of Bartholomé Mitre, publishes a cheap uniform edition, which is formed of some Argentine reprints and originals, but chiefly of French and English translations. The latest publication is advertised on the front page of the newspaper, and one often runs across "old friends" whose "new faces" cause a momentary check to the memory; such as *La Feria de Vanidades*, the identity of which is clear when one reads that the author is Thackeray. This "Biblioteca de la Nacion" is poorly got up and printed on wretched paper, but seems fairly widely read, and will doubtless stimulate the scarcely existent literary side of the Argentine, and in due time bear fruit. Translations of Nick Carter and the "penny dreadfuls" are rife, but a native writer, Gutierrez, who wrote in the seventies and eighties, created a national hero, Juan Moreira, who was a benevolent Billy the Kid. Gutierrez wrote many "dramas policiales," which are well worth reading for the light they throw in their side touches on "gaucho" life of those days.

Argentines are justifiably proud of Bartholomé Mitre, their historian soldier, who was twice president; and of Sarmiento, essayist and orator, who was also president, and who introduced the educational reforms whose application he had studied in the United States. At an auction in New York we secured a presentation copy of his *Vida de Lincoln*, written and published in this country in 1866. Mitre first published his history of General Belgrano, of revolutionary fame, in two volumes in 1859. It has run through many editions; the much enlarged one in four volumes is probably more universally seen in private houses than any other Argentine book. The first edition is now very rare and worth between forty and fifty dollars; but in a cheap Italian stationery-store we found a copy in excellent condition and paid for it only four dollars and fifty cents. The edition of 1887 brings anywhere from twenty to thirty dollars. Many copies were offered at sales, but we delayed in hopes of a better bargain, and one night our patience was rewarded. It was at the fag end of a private auction of endless rooms of cheap and tawdry furniture that the voluble auctioneer at length reached the contents of the solitary bookcase. Our coveted copy was knocked down to us at eight dollars

In native houses one very rarely finds what we would even dignify by the name of library. Generally a fair-sized bookcase of ill-assorted volumes is regarded as such. There are, however, excellent legal and medical collections to be seen, and Doctor Moreno's colonial quinta, with its well-filled shelves, chiefly volumes of South American exploration and development from the earliest times, forms a marked exception—an oasis in the desert. We once went to stay in the country with some Argentines, who seeing us arrive with books in our hands, proudly offered the use of their library, to which we had often heard their friends make reference. For some time we were greatly puzzled as to the location of this much-talked-of collection, and were fairly staggered on having a medium-sized bookcase, half of which was taken up by a set of excerpts from the "world's great thinkers and speakers," in French, pointed out as "the library."

As a rule the first thing a family will part with is its books. There are two sorts of auctions—judicial and booksellers'. The latter class are held by dealers who are having bad times and hope to liquidate some of their stock, but there are always cappers in the crowd who keep bidding until a book is as high and often higher than its market price. The majority of the books are generally legal or medical; and there is always a good number of young students who hope to get reference books cheaply. Most of the books are in Spanish, but there is a sprinkling of French, and often a number of English, German, and Portuguese, though these last are no more common in Argentina than are Spanish books in Brazil. At one auction there were a number of Portuguese lots which went for far more than they would have brought in Rio or São Paulo. Translations from the Portuguese are infrequent; the only ones we can recall were of Camões and Eça de Queiroz. In Brazil the only translation from Spanish we met with was of *Don Quixote*.

English books generally go reasonably at auctions. We got a copy of Page's *Paraguay and the River Plate* for twenty-five cents, but on another occasion had some very sharp bidding for Wilcox's *History of Our Colony in the River Plate*, London, 1807, written during the brief period when Buenos Ayres was an English possession. It was finally knocked down to us at twelve dollars; and after the auction our opponent offered us twice what he had let us have it for; we don't yet know what it is worth. The question of values is a difficult one, for there is little or no data to go upon; in consequence, the element of chance is very considerable. From several sources in the book world, we heard a wild and most improbable tale of how Quaritch and several other London houses had many years ago sent a consignment of books to be auctioned in the Argentine; and that the night of the auction was so cold and disagreeable that the exceedingly problematical buyers were still further reduced. The auction was held in spite of conditions, and rare incunabula are reported to have gone at a dollar apiece.

There was one judicial auction that lasted for the best part of a week—the entire stock of a large bookstore that had failed. They were mostly new books, and such old ones as were of any interest were interspersed in lots of ten or more of no value. The attendance was large and bidding was high. To get the few books we wanted we had also to buy a lot of waste material; but when we took this to a small and heretofore barren bookstore to exchange, we found a first edition of the three first volumes of *Kosmos*, for which, with a number of Portuguese and Spanish books thrown in, we made the exchange. We searched long and without success for the fourth volume, but as the volumes were published at long intervals, it is probable that the former owner had only possessed the three.

Our best finds were made not at auctions but in bookstores— often in little combination book, cigar, and stationery shops. We happened upon one of these latter one Saturday noon on our way to lunch at a little Italian restaurant, where you watched your chicken being most deliciously roasted on a spit before you. Chickens were forgotten, and during two hours' breathless hunting we found many good things, among them a battered old copy of Byron's poems, which had long since lost its binding. Pasted in it was the following original letter of Byron's, which as far as we know has never before been published:[1]

A Monsieur,
  Monsieur Galignani,
    18 Rue Vivienne,
      Paris.

Sir: In various numbers of your journal I have seen mentioned a work entitled *The Vampire*, with the addition of my name as that of the author. I am not the author, and never heard of the work in question until now. In a more recent paper I perceive a formal annunciation of *The Vampire*, with the addition of an account of my "residence in the Island of Mitylane," an island which I have occasionally sailed by in the course of travelling some years ago through the Levant—and where I should have no objection to reside—but where I have never yet resided. Neither of these performances are mine—and I presume that it is neither unjust nor ungracious to request that you will favour me by contradicting the advertisement to which I allude. If the book is clever, it would be base to deprive the real writer—whoever he may be—of his honours—and if stupid I desire the responsibility of nobody's dulness but my own. You will excuse the trouble I give you—the imputation is of no great importance—and as long as it was confined to surmises and reports—I should have received it as I have received many others—in silence. But the formality of a public advertisement of a book I never wrote, and a residence where I never resided—is a little too much—particularly as I have no notion of the contents of the one—nor the incidents of the other. I have besides a personal dislike to "vampires," and the little acquaintance I have with them would by no means induce me to divulge their secrets. You did me a much less injury by your paragraphs about "my devotion" and "abandonment of society for the sake of religion"—which appeared in your *Messenger* during last Lent—all of which are not founded on fact—but you see I do not contradict them, because they are merely personal, whereas the others in some degree concern the reader. . . .

You will oblige me by complying with my request for contradiction. I assure you that I know nothing of the work or works in question — and have the honour to be (as the correspondents to magazines say) "your constant reader" and very

obedt

humble Servt,

BYRON.

To the editor of *Galignani's Messenger.* Etc., etc., etc.
Venice, April 27, 1819.

Curiously enough, the book itself had been published by Galignani in 1828. The cost of our total purchases, a goodly heap, amounted to but five dollars.

The balance in quantity if not in quality in old books is held in Buenos Ayres by three brothers named Palumbo — Italians. The eldest is a surly old man who must be treated with severity from the very beginning. How he manages to support himself we do not know, for whenever we were in his store we were sure to hear him assail some customer most abusively. In a small subsidiary store of his, among a heap of old pamphlets, we came upon the original folios of Humboldt's account of the fauna and flora of South America. Upon asking the price, the man said thirty-five apiece — we thought he meant pesos, and our surprise was genuine when we found he meant centavos — about fifteen cents. From him we got the first edition of Kendall's *Santa Fé Expedition.* One of his brothers was very pleasant and probably, in consequence, the most prosperous of the three. The third was reputed crazy, and certainly acted so, but after an initial encounter we became friends and got on famously. All three had a very fair idea of the value of Argentine books, but knew little or nothing about English.

Another dealer who has probably a better stock than any of the Palumbos is a man named Real y Taylor. His grandmother was English, and his father spent his life dealing in books. At his death the store was closed and the son started speculating in land with the money his father had left him. Prices soared and he bought, but when the crash came he was caught with many others. Bethinking himself of his father's books, he took them out of storage and opened a small booth. The stock was large and a good part of it has not yet been unpacked. Taylor has only a superficial knowledge of what he deals in. He shears folios, strips off original boards and old leathers to bind in new pasteboard, and raises the price five or ten dollars after the process. In this he is no different from the rest, for after a fairly comprehensive experience in Buenos Ayres we may give it as our opinion that there is not a single dealer who knows the "rules" as they are observed by scores of dealers in America and England. Taylor had only one idea, and that was that if any one were interested in a book, that book must be of great value; he would name a ridiculous price, and it was a question of weeks and months before he would reduce it to anything within the bounds of reason. We never really got very much from him, the best things being several old French books of early voyages to South America and a first edition of Anson's *Voyage Around the World*. Just before we left he decided to auction off his stock, putting up five hundred lots a month. The first auction lasted three nights. The catalogue was amusing, giving a description of each book in bombastic fashion — all were "unique in interest," and about every third was the "only copy extant outside the museums." He had put base prices on most, and for the rest had arranged with cappers. The attendance was very small and nearly everything was bid in. It was curious to see how to the last he held that any book that any one was interested in must be of unusual worth. There was put up a French translation of Azara's *Quadrupeds of Paraguay*. The introduction was by Cuvier, but it was not of great interest to us, for a friend had given us the valuable original Spanish edition. Taylor had asked fifteen dollars, which we had regarded as out of the question; he then took off the original binding, cut and colored the pages, and rebound it, asking twenty dollars. At the auction we thought we would get it, if it went for very little; but when we bid, Taylor got up and told the auctioneer to say that as it was a work of unique value he had put as base price fifteen dollars each for the two volumes. The auction was a failure, and as it had been widely and expensively advertised, the loss must have been considerable.

As a whole, we found the booksellers of a disagreeable temperament. In one case we almost came to blows; luckily not until we had looked over the store thoroughly and bought all we really wanted, among them a first edition of Howells's *Italian Journeys*, in perfect condition, for twenty-five cents. There were, of course, agreeable exceptions, such as the old French-Italian from whom, after many months' intermittent bargaining, we bought Le Vaillant's *Voyage en Afrique*, the first edition, with most delightful steel-engravings. He at first told us he was selling it at a set price on commission, which is what we found they often said when they thought you wanted a book and wished to preclude bargaining. This old man had Amsterdam catalogues that he consulted in regard to prices when, as could not have been often the case, he found in them references to books he had in stock. We know of no Argentine old bookstore that prints a catalogue.

In the larger provincial cities of Argentina we met with singularly little success. In Cordoba the only reward of an eager search was a battered paper-covered copy of *All on the Irish Shore*, with which we were glad to renew an acquaintance that had lapsed for several years. We had had such high hopes of Cordoba, as being the old university town and early centre of learning! There was indeed one trail that seemed to promise well, and we diligently pursued vague stories of a "viejo" who had trunks of old books in every language, but when we eventually found his rooms, opening off a dirty little patio, they were empty and bereft; and we learned from a grimy brood of children that he had gone to the hospital in Buenos Ayres and died there, and that his boxes had been taken away by they knew not whom.

As in Argentina, the best-known Chilian writers are historians or lawyers; and in our book-hunts in Santiago we encountered more or less the same conditions that held in Buenos Ayres—shelf upon shelf of legal or medical reference books and technical treatises. The works of certain well-known historians, such as Vicuña Mackenna and Amonategui, consistently command relatively high prices; but, as a whole, books are far cheaper on the west side of the Andes. One long afternoon in the Calle San Diego stands out. It was a rich find, but we feel that the possibilities of that store are still unexhausted. That afternoon's trove included the first edition of Mungo Park's *Travels*, with the delightful original etchings; a *History of Guatemala*, written by the Dominican missionaries, published in 1619, an old leather-bound folio, in excellent shape; a first edition of Holmes's *Autocrat of the Breakfast-Table* and three of the eight volumes of *State Papers and Publick Documents of the United States*. In these last there was James Monroe's book-plate, and it was curious to imagine how these volumes from his library had found their way to a country where his "doctrine" has been the subject of such bitter discussion and so much misinterpretation. The value of the original covers was no more understood in Chile than in Argentina, and we got a complete set of Vicuña Mackenna's *Campaña de Tacna* in the original pamphlets, as published, for but half what was currently asked for bound and mutilated copies.

Valparaiso proved a barren field, and although one of the chief delights in book-hunting lies in the fact that you can never feel that you have completely exhausted the possibilities of a place, we came nearer to feeling that way about Valparaiso than we ever had about a town before. We found but one store that gave any promise, and from it all we got were the first seven volumes of Dickens's *Household Words* in perfect condition, and the *Campaign of the Rapidan*.

The little coast towns of Chile and Peru are almost as barren as the desert rocks and sand-hills that surround them; but even here we had occasional surprises, as when we picked up for fifty cents, at Antofogasta, a desolate, thriving little mining-port in the north of Chile, Vicuña Mackenna's *Life of O'Higgins*, for which the current price is from ten to fifteen dollars. Another time, in Coquimbo, we saw a man passing along the street with a hammered-copper bowl that we coveted, and following, we found him the owner of a junk-shop filled with a heterogeneous collection of old clothes, broken and battered furniture, horse-trappings, and a hundred and one odds and ends, among which were scattered some fifty or sixty books. One of these was a first edition of Hawthorne's *Twice-Told Tales* in the familiar old brown boards of Ticknor & Company.

Our South American book-hunting ended in Lima, the entrancing old city of the kings, once the capital of the New World, and not yet robbed by this commercial age of all its glamour and backwardness. We expected much, knowing that when the Chilians occupied the city in 1880 they sacked the national library of fifty thousand volumes that their own liberator, San Martin, had founded in 1822, and although many of the books were carried off to Chile, the greater part was scattered around Lima or sold by weight on the streets. We shall always feel that with more time, much patience, and good luck we could have unearthed many treasures; although at first sight the field is not a promising one, and, as elsewhere, one's acquaintances assure one that there is nothing to be found. In spite of this, however, we came upon a store that appeared teeming with possibilities. Without the "flaire" or much luck it might be passed by many times without exciting interest. Over the dingy grated window of a dilapidated colonial house is the legend "Encuadernacion y Imprenta" ("Binding and Printing.") Through the grimy window-panes may be seen a row of dull law-books; but if you open the big gate and cross the patio, with its ancient hand-well in the centre, on the opposite side are four or five rooms with shelves of books along the walls and tottering and fallen piles of books scattered over the floor. Here we picked up among others an amusing little old vellum-covered edition of Horace, printed in England in 1606, which must have early found its way to South America, to judge from the Spanish scrawls on the title-page. We also got many of the works of Ricardo Palma, Peru's most famous writer, who built up the ruined national library, which now possesses some sixty thousand volumes, of which a twelfth part were donated by our own Smithsonian Institution. One of the volumes we bought had been given by Palma to a friend, and had an autograph dedication which in other countries would have greatly enhanced its value, but which, curiously enough, seems to make no difference in South America. In Buenos Ayres we got a copy of the *Letters from Europe* of Campos Salles, Brazil's greatest president, which had been inscribed by him to the Argentine translator. Once in São Paulo we picked up an autographed copy of Gomes de Amorim, and in neither case did the autograph enter into the question of determining the price.

We had heard rumors of possibilities in store for us in Ecuador, Colombia, and Venezuela, but Lima was our "farthest north," for there our ramblings in South America were reluctantly brought to a close. We feel, however, that such as they were, and in spite of the fact that the names of many of the authors and places will be strange to our brethren who have confined their explorations to the northern hemisphere, these notes may awaken interest in a little-known field, which, if small in comparison with America or the Old World, offers at times unsuspected prizes and rewards.

CHAPTER VI

SETH BULLOCK — SHERIFF OF THE BLACK HILLS COUNTRY

WITH the death of Captain Seth Bullock, of Deadwood, South Dakota, there came to us who were his friends not only a deep sense of personal loss, but also the realization that one of the very last of the old school of frontiersmen had gone, one of those whom Lowell characterized as "stern men with empires in their brains." The hard hand of circumstance called forth and developed the type, and for a number of generations the battle with the wilderness continued in bitter force, and a race was brought forth trained to push on far beyond the "edge of cultivation," and contend in his remote fastnesses with the Red Indian, and eke out a hard-earned existence from the grim and resentful wilds. In the wake of the vanguard came the settler and after him the merchant, and busy towns sprang up where the lonely camp-fire of the pioneer had flared to the silent forest. The restless blood of the frontiers pressed ever onward; the Indian melted away like "snow upon the desert's dusty face"; the great herds of game that formerly blackened the plains left the mute testimony of their passing in the scattered piles of whitened skulls and bleached bones. At last the tune came when there was no further frontier to conquer. The restless race of empire-makers had staring them in the face the same fate as the Indian. Their rough-and-ready justice administered out of hand had to give way before the judge with his court-house and his jury. The majority of the old Indian fighters were shouldered aside and left to end their days as best they could, forgotten by those for whom they had won the country. They could not adapt themselves to the new existence; their day had passed and they went to join the Indian and the buffalo.

Captain Seth Bullock, however, belonged to the minority, for no turn of the wheel could destroy his usefulness to the community, and his large philosophy of the plains enabled him to fit into and hold his place through every shift of surroundings. The Captain's family came from Virginia, but he was born in Windsor, Ontario, in 1849. Before he was twenty he had found his way to Montana, and built for himself a reputation for justice which at that day and in that community could only be established by cold and dauntless courage.

One of the feats of his early days of which he was justly proud was when he had himself hung the first man to be hung by law in Montana. The crowd of prospectors and cow-punchers did not approve of such an unusual, unorthodox method of procedure as the hanging of a man by a public hangman after he had been duly tried and sentenced. They wished to take the prisoner and string him up to the nearest tree or telegraph-pole, with the readiness and despatch to which they were accustomed. To evidence their disapproval they started to shoot at the hangman; he fled, but before the crowd could secure their victim, the Captain had the mastery of the situation, and, quieting his turbulent fellow citizens with a cold eye and relentless six-shooter, he himself performed the task that the hangman had left unfinished. The incident inspired the mob with a salutary respect for the law and its ability to carry out its sentences. I do not remember whether the Captain was mayor or sheriff at the time. He was trusted and admired as well as feared, and when he was barely twenty-two he was elected State senator from Helena, the largest town in the then territory of Montana.

It was in 1876 that the Captain first went to the Black Hills, that lovely group of mountains in the southwestern corner of South Dakota. He came with the first rush of prospectors when the

The Captain makes advances to a little Indian girl

famous Hidden Treasure Mine was discovered. On the site of what is at present the town of Deadwood he set up a store for miners' supplies, and soon had established himself as the arm of the law in that very lawless community. That was the Captain's rôle all through his life. In the early years he would spend day and night in the saddle in pursuit of rustlers and road-agents. When he once started on the trail nothing could make him relinquish it; and when he reached the end, his quarry would better surrender without drawing. He had a long arm and his district was known throughout the West as an unhealthy place for bad men. Starting as federal peace officer of the Black Hills, hc later became marshal and sheriff of the district, and eventually marshal of South Dakota, which position he held until 1914. As years passed and civilization advanced, his bag of malefactors became less simple in character, although maintaining some of the old elements. In 1908 he wrote me:

I have been very busy lately; pulled two horse thieves from Montana last week for stealing horses from the Pine Ridge Indians. I leave to-day for Leavenworth with a bank cashier for mulling a bank. He may turn up on Wall Street when his term expires, to take a post graduate course.

In 1907 he told me that he was going off among the Ute Indians, and I asked him to get me some of their pipes. He answered: "The Utes are not pipe-makers; they spend all their time rustling and eating government grub. We had six horse-thieves for the pen after the past term of court, and should get four more at the June term in Pierre. This will keep them quiet for a while. I am now giving my attention to higher finance, and have one of the Napoleons—a bank president—in jail here. He only got away with $106,000—he did not have time to become eligible for the Wall Street class."

It was when the Captain was sheriff of the Black Hills that father first met him. A horsethief that was "wanted" in the Deadwood district managed to slip out of the Captain's clutches and was captured by father, who was deputy sheriff in a country three or four hundred miles north. A little while later father had to go to Deadwood on business. Fording a river some miles out of town he ran into the Captain. Father had often heard of Seth Bullock, for his record and character were known far and wide, and he had no difficulty in identifying the tall, slim, hawk-featured Westerner sitting his horse like a centaur. Seth Bullock, however, did not know so much about father, and was very suspicious of the rough, unkempt group just in from two weeks' sleeping out in the gumbo and sage-brush. He made up his mind that it was a tin-horn gambling outfit and would bear close watching. He was not sure but what it would be best to turn them right back, and let them walk around his district "like it was a swamp." After settling father's identity the Captain's suspicions vanished. That was the beginning of their lifelong friendship.

After father had returned to the East to live, Seth Bullock would come on to see him every so often, and whenever my father's campaigning took him West the Captain would join the train and stay with him until the trip was finished. These tours were rarely without incident, and in his autobiography father has told of the part Seth Bullock played on one of them.

When, in 1900, I was nominated for Vice-President, I was sent by the National Committee on a trip into the States of the high plains and the Rocky Mountains. These had all gone overwhelmingly for Mr. Bryan on the free-silver issue four years previously, and it was thought that I, because of my knowledge of and acquaintanceship with the people, might accomplish something toward bringing them back into line. It was an interesting trip, and the monotony usually attendant upon such a campaign of political speaking was diversified in vivid fashion by occasional hostile audiences. One or two of the meetings ended in riots. One meeting was finally broken up by a mob; everybody fought so that the speaking had to stop. Soon after this we reached another town where we were told there might be trouble. Here the local committee included an old and valued friend, a "two-gun" man of repute, who was not in the least quarrelsome, but who always kept his word. We marched round to the local opera-house, which was packed with a mass of men, many of them rather rough-looking. My friend the two-gun man sat immediately behind me, a gun on each hip, his arms folded, looking at the audience; fixing his gaze with instant intentness on any section of the house from which there came so much as a whisper. The audience listened to me with rapt attention. At the end, with a pride in my rhetorical powers which proceeded from a misunderstanding of the situation, I remarked to the chairman: "I held that audience well; there wasn't an interruption." To which the chairman replied: "Interruption? Well, I guess not! Seth had sent round word that if any son of a gun peeped he'd kill him." (*Autobiography*, p. 141.)

Father had the greatest admiration and affection for the Captain. It was to him that he was referring in his autobiography when he wrote:

I have sometimes been asked if Wister's *Virginian* is not overdrawn; why, one of the men I have mentioned in this chapter was in all essentials the "Virginian" in real life, not only in his force but in his charm.

When we were hunting in Africa father decided that he would try to get Seth Bullock to meet us in Europe at the end of the trip. I remember father describing him to some of our English friends in Khartoum, and saying: "Seth Bullock is a true Westerner, the finest type of frontiersman. He could handle himself in any situation, and if I felt that I did not wish him to meet any particular person, the reflection would be entirely on the latter."

The Captain wrote me that he was afraid he could not meet us in London because of the illness of one of his daughters, but matters eventually worked out in such a way that he was able to go over to England, and when he met father there he said he felt like hanging his Stetson on the dome of Saint Paul's and shooting it off, to show his exhilaration at the reunion. He thoroughly enjoyed himself in England, and while at bottom he was genuinely appreciative of the Britisher, he could not help poking sly fun at him. I remember riding on a bus with him and hearing him ask the conductor where this famous Picalilly Street was. The conductor said: "You must mean Piccadilly, sir." The Captain entered into a lengthy conversation with him, and with an unmoved stolidity of facial expression that no Red Indian could have bettered, referred each time to "Picalilly," and each time the little bus conductor would interpose a "You mean Piccadilly, sir," with the dogged persistency of his race.

The major-domos and lackeys at the Guild-hall and other receptions and the "beefeaters" at the Tower were a never-failing source of delight; he would try to picture them on a bad pony in the cow country, and explain that their costume would "make them the envy of every Sioux brave at an Indian dog-dance."

When my sister and I were in Edinburgh, the local guide who took us through the Castle showed us an ancient gun, which instead of being merely double-barrelled, possessed a cluster of five or six barrels. With great amusement he told us how an American to whom he had been showing the piece a few days previously had remarked that to be shot at with that gun must be like taking a shower-bath. A few questions served to justify the conclusion we had immediately formed as to identity of our predecessor.

The summer that I was fourteen father shipped me off to the Black Hills for a camping trip with Seth Bullock. I had often seen him in the East, so the tall, spare figure and the black Stetson were familiar to me when the Captain boarded the train a few stations before reaching Deadwood. Never shall I forget the romance of that first trip in the West. It was all new to me. Unfortunately I had to leave for the East for the start of school before the opening of the deer season; but we caught a lot of trout, and had some unsuccessful bear-hunts — hunts which were doomed to unsuccess before they started, but which supplied the requisite thrill notwithstanding. All we ever found of the bear was their tracks, but we had a fleeting glimpse of a bobcat, and that was felt amply to repay any amount of tramping. Our bag consisted of one jack-rabbit. The Captain told us that we were qualified to join a French trapper whom he had known. The Frenchman was caught by an unusually early winter and snowed in away off in the hills. In the spring, a good deal to every one's surprise, he turned up, looking somewhat thin, but apparently totally unconcerned over his forced hibernation. When asked what he had lived on, he replied: "Some day I keel two jack-rabeet, one day one, one day none!"

The Captain and I took turns at writing my diary. I find his entry for August 26:

Broke camp at Jack Boyden's on Sand Creek at 6.30 A. M., and rode via Redwater Valley and Hay Creek to Belle Fourche, arriving at the S. B. ranch at two o'clock; had lunch of cold cabbage; visited the town; returned to camp at five P. M.; had supper at the wagon and fought mosquitoes until ten o'clock.

Broke camp and rode via Owl Creek divide and Indian Creek through several very large towns inhabited chiefly by prairie dogs, to our camp on Porcupine Creek. Fought mosquitoes from 3 A. M. to breakfast time.

I had long been an admirer of Bret Harte, and many of the people I met might have stepped from the pages of his stories. There was the old miner with twenty-two children, who couldn't remember all their names. His first wife had presented him with ten of them, but when he married again he had told his second wife that it was his initial venture in matrimony. He gave a vivid description of the scene when some of the progeny of his first marriage unexpectedly put in an appearance. Time had smoothed things over, and the knowledge of her predecessor had evidently only acted as a spur to greater deeds, as exemplified in the twelve additions to the family.

Then there was the old lady with the vinegar jug. She was the postmistress of Buckhorn. We had some difficulty in finding the post-office, but at length we learned that the postmistress had moved it fifteen miles away, to cross the State border, in order that she might live in Wyoming and have a vote. We reached the shack to find it deserted, but we had not long to wait before she rode in, purple in the face and nearly rolling off her pony from laughter. She told us that she had got some vinegar from a friend, and while she was riding along the motion exploded the jug, and the cork hit her in the head; what with the noise and the blow she made sure the Indians were after her, and rode for her life a couple of miles before she realized what had happened.

What could have surpassed the names of the trails along which we rode and the canyons in which we camped? There was Hidden Treasure Gulch and Calamity Hollow, and a score more equally satisfying. That first trip was an immense success, and all during the winter that followed whenever school life became particularly irksome I would turn to plans for the expedition that we had scheduled for the next summer.

When the time to leave for the West arrived I felt like an old stager, and indulged for the first time in the delight of getting out my hunting outfit, deciding what I needed, and supplementing my last summer's rig with other things that I had found would be useful. Like all beginners I imagined that I required a lot for which I had in reality no possible use. Some men always set off festooned like Christmas-trees, and lose half the pleasure of the trip through trying to keep track of their belongings. They have special candles, patented lanterns, enormous jack-knives with a blade to fulfil every conceivable purpose, rifles and revolvers and shotguns galore; almost anything that comes under the classification of "it might come in handy." The more affluent hunter varies only in the quality and not the quantity of his "gadgets." He usually has each one neatly tucked away in a pigskin case. The wise man, however, soon learns that although anything may "come in handy" once on a trip, you could even on that occasion either get along without it or find a substitute that would do almost as well. It is surprising with what a very little one can make out perfectly comfortably. This was a lesson which I very quickly learned from the Captain.

The second trip that we took was from Deadwood, South Dakota, to Medora, North Dakota. I had never seen the country in which father ranched, and Seth Bullock decided to take me up along the trail that father had been travelling when they met for the first time.

We set off on Friday the 13th, and naturally everything that happened was charged up to that inauspicious day. We lost all our horses the first night, and only succeeded in retrieving a part of them. Thereafter it started in raining, and the gumbo mud became all but impassable for the "chuck-wagon." The mosquitoes added to our misery, and I find in my diary in the Captain's handwriting a note to the effect that "Paul shot three mosquitoes with a six-shooter. Stanley missed with a shotgun."

The Captain was as stolid and unconcerned as a Red Indian through every change of weather. He had nicknamed me "Kim" from Kipling's tale, and after me he had named a large black horse which he always rode. It was an excellent animal with a very rapid walk which proved the bane of my existence. My pony, "Pickpocket," had no pace that corresponded, and to adapt himself was forced to travel at a most infernal jiggle that was not only exceedingly wearing but shook me round so that the rain permeated in all sorts of crevices which might reasonably have been expected to prove water-tight. With the pride of a boy on his second trip, I could not bring myself to own up to my discomfort. If I had, the Captain would have instantly changed his pace; but it seemed a soft and un-Western admission to make, so I suffered in external silence, while inwardly heaping every insult I could think of upon the Captain's mount. We were travelling long distances, so the gait was rarely changed unless I made some excuse to loiter behind, and then walked my pony in slow and solitary comfort until the Captain was almost out of sight, and it was time to press into a lope which comfortably and far too rapidly once more put me even with him.

The Captain was a silent companion; he would ride along hour after hour, chewing a long black cigar, in a silence broken only by verses he would hum to himself. There was one that went on interminably, beginning:

> "I wonder if ever a cowboy
> Will be seen in those days long to come;
> I wonder if ever an Indian
> Will be seen in that far bye-and-bye."

Every now and then some butte would suggest a reminiscence of the early days, and a few skilfully directed questions would lure him into a chain of anecdotes of the already vanished border-life. He was continually coming out with a quotation from some author with whose writings I had never thought him acquainted. Fishing in a Black Hills stream, I heard him mutter:

> "So you heard the left fork of the Yuba
> As you stood on the banks of the Po."

He had read much of Kipling's prose and poetry, but what he most often quoted were the lines to Fighting Bob Evans.

In his house in Deadwood he had a good library, the sort of one which made you feel that the books had been selected to read and enjoy, and not bought by the yard like window-curtains, or any other furnishings thought necessary for a house. Mrs. Bullock was president of the "Women's Literary Club," and I remember father being much impressed with the work that she was doing.

As I have said before, the Captain was a man whom changing conditions could not throw to one side. He would anticipate the changes, and himself take the lead in them, adapting himself to the new conditions; you could count upon finding him on top. He was very proud of the fact that he had brought the first alfalfa to the State, and showed me his land near Belle Fourche, where he had planted the original crop. Its success was immediate. He said that he could not claim the credit of having introduced potatoes, but an old friend of his was entitled to the honor, and he delighted in telling the circumstances. The Captain's friend, whom we can call Judge Jones, for I've forgotten his name, had opened a trading-post in what was at that time the wild territory of Dakota. The Indians were distinctly hostile, and at any good opportunity were ready to raid the posts, murdering the factors and looting the trading goods. In the judge's territory there was one particularly ugly customer, half Indian and half negro, known as Nigger Bill. The judge was much interested in the success of his adventure in potatoes, and the following was one of the letters he received from his factor, as Seth Bullock used to quote it to me:

DEAR JUDGE,

This is to tell you all is well here and I hope is same with you. Nigger Bill came to the door of the stockade to-day and said "I am going to get in." I said "Nigger Bill you will not get in." Nigger Bill said "I will get in." I shot Nigger Bill. He is dead. The potatoes is doing fine.

Although realizing to the full that the change was inevitable and, of course, to the best interests of the country, and naturally taking much pride in the progress his State was making, the Captain could not help at times feeling a little melancholy over the departed days when there was no wire in the country, and one could ride where one listed. He wrote me in 1911: "The part of South Dakota which you knew has all been covered with the shacks of homesteaders, from Belle Fourche to Medora, and from the Cheyenne agency to the Creek Where the Old Woman Died." The old times had gone, never to return, and although the change was an advance, it closed an existence that could never be forgotten or relived by those who had taken part in it.

The Captain gave me very sound advice when I was trying to make up my mind whether or not to go to college. I was at the time going through the period of impatience that comes to so many boys when they feel that they are losing valuable time, during which they should be starting in to make their way in the world. I had talked it over with the Captain during one of the summer trips, and soon afterward he wrote me:

Ride the old studies with spurs. I don't like the idea of your going out to engage in business until you have gone through Harvard. You will have plenty of time after you have accomplished this to tackle the world. Take my advice, my boy, and don't think of it. A man without a college education nowadays is badly handicapped. If he has had the opportunity to go through college and does not take advantage of it, he goes through life with a regret that becomes more intensified as he gets older. Life is a very serious proposition if we would live it well.

I went through college and I have often realized since how excellent this advice was, and marvelled not a little at the many-sidedness of a frontiersman who could see that particular situation so clearly.

The year before I went with my father to Africa, R. H. Munro Ferguson and myself joined the Captain in South Dakota for a prairie-chicken hunt. We were to shoot in the vicinity of the Cheyenne Indian reservation, and the Captain took us through the reservation to show us how the Indian question was being handled. The court was excellently run, but what impressed us most was the judge's name, for he was called Judge No Heart. Some of our hunting companions rejoiced in equally unusual names. There were Spotted Rabbit, No Flesh, Yellow Owl, and High Hawk, not to forget Spotted Horses, whose prolific wife was known as Mrs. Drops-Two-at-a-Time. We had with us another man named Dave Snowball, who looked and talked just like a Southern darky. As a matter of fact, he was half negro and half Indian. In the old days negro slaves not infrequently escaped and joined the Indians. I went to see Dave's father. There was no mistaking him for what he was, but when I spoke to him he would answer me in Sioux and the only English words I could extract from him were "No speak

A morning's bag of prairie chicken in South Dakota
Seth Bullock is second from the left, and R. H. Munro Ferguson third

English." He may have had some hazy idea that if he talked English some one would arrest him and send him back to his old masters, although they had probably been dead for thirty or forty years. Possibly living so long among the Sioux, he had genuinely forgotten the language of his childhood.

High Hawk and Oliver Black Hawk were old "hostiles." So was Red Bear. We came upon him moving house. The tepee had just been dismantled, and the support poles were being secured to a violently objecting pony. A few weeks later when we were on the train going East, Frederic Remington joined us. He was returning from Montana, and upon hearing that we had been on the Cheyenne reservation he asked if we had run into old Red Bear, who had once saved his life. He told us that many years before he had been picked up by a party of hostiles, and they had determined to give him short shrift, when Red Bear, with whom he had previously struck a friendship, turned up, and successfully interceded with his captors. One reminiscence led to another, and we were soon almost as grateful to Red Bear for having opened such a store as Remington had been for having his life spared. Frederic Remington was a born raconteur, and pointed his stories with a bluff, homely philosophy, redolent of the plains and the sage-brush.

The night before we left the Indians the Captain called a council. All the old "hostiles" and many of the younger generation gathered. The peace-pipes circulated. We had brought with us from New York a quantity of German porcelain pipes to trade with the Indians. Among them was one monster with a bowl that must have held from an eighth to a quarter of a pound of tobacco. The Indians ordinarily smoke "kinnikinick," which is chopped-up willow bark. It is mild and gives a pleasant, aromatic smoke. The tobacco which we had was a coarse, strong shag. We filled the huge pipe with it, and, lighting it, passed it round among the silent, solemn figures grouped about the fire. The change was as instantaneous as it was unpremeditated. The first "brave" drew deeply and inhaled a few strong puffs; with a choking splutter he handed the pipe to his nearest companion. The scene was repeated, and as each Indian, heedless of the fate of his comrades, inhaled the smoke of the strong shag, he would break out coughing, until the pipe had completed the circuit and the entire group was coughing in unison. Order was restored and willow bark substituted for tobacco, with satisfactory results. Then we each tried our hand at speaking. One by one the Indians took up the thread, grunting out their words between puffs. The firelight rose and fell, lighting up the shrouded shapes. When my turn came I spoke through an interpreter. Coached by the Captain as to what were their most lamentable failings—those that most frequently were the means of his making their acquaintance—I gave a learned discourse upon the evils of rustling ponies, and the pleasant life that lay before those who abstained from doing so. Grunts of approval, how sincere I know not, were the gratifying reply to my efforts. The powwow broke up with a substantial feast of barbecued sheep, and next morning we left our nomadic hosts to continue their losing fight to maintain their hereditary form of existence, hemmed in by an ever-encroaching white man's civilization.

Near the reservation we came upon two old outlaw buffaloes, last survivors of the great herds that not so many years previously had roamed these plains, providing food and clothing for the Indians until wiped out by the ruthless white man. These two bulls, living on because they were too old and tough for any one to bother about, were the last survivors left in freedom. A few days later we were shown by Scottie Phillips over his herd. He had many pure breeds but more hybrids, and the latter looked the healthier. Scottie had done a valuable work in preserving these buffalo. He was a squaw-man, and his pleasant Indian wife gave us excellent buffalo-berry preserves that she had put up.

Scottie's ranch typified the end of both buffalo and Indian. Before a generation is past the buffalo will survive only in the traces of it left by crossing with cattle; and the same fate eventually awaits the Indian. No matter how wise be the course followed in governing the remnants of the Indian race, it can only be a question of time before their individuality sinks and they are absorbed.

The spring following this expedition I set off with father for Africa. The Captain took a great deal of interest in the plans for the trip. A week before we sailed he wrote:

I send you to-day by American Express the best gun I know of for you to carry when in Africa. It is a single action Colts 38 on a heavy frame. It is a business weapon, always reliable, and will shoot where you hold it. When loaded, carry it on the safety, or first cock of the hammer.

Seth Bullock was a hero-worshipper and father was his great hero. It would have made no difference what father did or said, the Captain would have been unshakably convinced without going into the matter at all that father was justified. There is an old adage that runs: "Any one can have friends that stand by him when he's right; what you want is friends that stand by you when you're wrong." Seth Bullock, had occasion ever demanded it, would have been one of the latter.

In the Cuban War he was unable to get into the Rough Riders, and so joined a cowboy regiment which was never fortunate enough to get over to Cuba, but suffered all its casualties—and there were plenty of them—from typhoid fever, in a camp somewhere in the South. He was made a sort of honorary member of the Rough Riders, and when there were informal reunions held in Washington he was counted upon to take part in them. He was a favorite with every one, from the White House ushers to the French Ambassador. As an honorary member of the Tennis Cabinet he was present at the farewell dinner held in the White House three days before father left the presidency. A bronze cougar by Proctor had been selected as a parting gift, and it was concealed under a mass of flowers in the centre of the table. The Captain had been chosen to make the presentation speech, and when he got up and started fumbling with flowers to disclose the cougar father could not make out what had happened.

The Captain, as he said himself, was a poor hand at saying good-by. He was in New York shortly before we sailed for Africa, but wrote: "I must leave here to-day for Sioux Falls; then again I am a mollycoddle when it comes to bidding good-by; can always easier write good-by than speak it."

His gloomy forebodings about the Brazilian trip were well justified. He was writing me to South America:

I was glad to hear you will be with your father. I have been uneasy about this trip of his, but now that I know you are along I will be better satisfied. I don't think much of that country you are to explore as a health resort, and there are no folks like home folks when one is sick.

The Captain made up his mind that if his regiment had failed to get into the Cuban War the same thing would not happen in the case of another war. In July, 1916, when the Mexican situation seemed even more acute than usual, I heard from the Captain:

If we have war with Mexico you and I will have to go. I am daily in receipt of application from the best riders in the country. Tell the Colonel I have carried out his plan for the forming of a regiment, and within fifteen days from getting word from him, will have a regiment for his division that will meet with his approval. You are to have a captaincy to start with. I don't think Wilson will fight without he is convinced it will aid in his election. He is like Artemus Ward—willing to sacrifice his wife's relations on the altar of his country.

The Mexican situation continued to drag along, but we at length entered the European war, and for a while it looked as if my father would be allowed to raise a division and take it over to the other side. The Captain had already the nucleus of his regiment, and the telegrams passed fast and furiously. However, for reasons best known to the authorities in Washington, it all turned out to be to no purpose. The Captain was enraged. He wrote me out to Mesopotamia, where I was serving in the British forces:

I was very much disgusted with Wilson when he turned us down. I had a splendid organization twelve hundred strong, comprising four hundred miners from the Black Hills Mines, four hundred railroad boys from the lines of the Chicago and Northwestern, and the C. B. and Q. in South Dakota, Western Nebraska, and Wyoming, and four hundred boys from the ranges of Western South Dakota, Montana, and Wyoming. It was the pick of the country. Your troop was especially good; while locally known as the Deadwood troop, most of the members were from the country northwest of Belle Fourche; twenty of your troop were Sioux who had served on the Indian police. Sixty-five per cent of the regiment had military training. Damn the dirty politics that kept us from going. I am busy now locally with the Red Cross and the Exemption Board of this county, being chairman of each. We will show the Democrats that we are thoroughbreds and will do our bit even if we are compelled to remain at home with the Democrats.

After expatiating at some length and with great wealth of detail as to just what he thought of the attitude of the administration, the Captain continued with some characteristic advice:

I am going to caution you now on being careful when you are on the firing line. Don't try for any Victoria Cross, or lead any forlorn hopes; modern war does not require these sacrifices, nor are battles won that way nowadays. I wouldn't have you fail in any particular of a brave American soldier, and I know you won't, but there is a vast difference between bravery and foolhardiness, and a man with folks at home is extremely selfish if unnecessarily foolhardy in the face of danger.

All of it very good, sound advice, and just such as the Captain might have been expected to give, but the last in the world that any one would have looked for him to personally follow.

The letter ended with "I think the war will be over this year. I did want to ride a spotted cayuse into Berlin, but it don't look now as if I would."

The next time that I heard from the Captain was some time after I had joined the American Expeditionary Forces in France. In characteristic fashion he addressed the letter merely "Care of General Pershing, France," and naturally the letter took three or four months before it finally reached me. The Captain had been very ill, but treated the whole matter as a joke.

I have just returned from California, where I was on the sick list since last December, six months in a hospital and sanitarium while the doctors were busy with knives, and nearly took me over the divide. I am recovering slowly, and hope to last till the Crown Prince and his murdering progenitor are hung. I was chairman of the Exemption Board in 1917 and stuck to it until I was taken ill with grippe, which ended in an intestinal trouble which required the services of two surgeons and their willing knives to combat. The folks came to California after the remains, but when they arrived they found the remains sitting up and cussing the Huns.

Now, Kim, take care of yourself; don't get reckless. Kill all the Huns you can, but don't let them have the satisfaction of getting you.

My father's death was a fearful blow to the old Captain. Only those who knew him well realized how hard he was hit. He immediately set to work to arrange some monument to my father's memory. With the native good taste that ever characterized him, instead of thinking in terms of statues, he decided that the dedication of a mountain would be most fitting, and determined to make the shaft to be placed upon its summit simple in both form and inscription. Father was the one honorary member of the Society of Black Hills Pioneers, and it was in conjunction with this society that the Captain arranged that Sheep Mountain, a few miles away from Deadwood, should be renamed Mount Roosevelt.

General Wood made the address. A number of my friends who were there gave me the latest news of the Captain. He wrote me that he expected to come East in September; that he was not feeling very fit, and that he was glad to have been able to go through with the dedication of the mountain. He was never a person to talk about himself, so I have no way of knowing, other than intuition, but I am certain that he felt all along that his days were numbered, and held on mainly in order to accomplish his purpose of raising the memorial.

I waited until the middle of September and then wrote to Deadwood to ask the Captain when he would be coming. I found the reply in the newspapers a few days later. The Captain was dead. The gallant old fellow had crossed the divide that he wrote about, leaving behind him not merely the sorrow of his friends but their pride in his memory. Well may we feel proud of having been numbered among the friends of such a thoroughgoing, upstanding American as Seth Bullock. As long as our country produces men of such caliber, we may face the future with a consciousness of our ability to win through such dark days as may confront us. The changes and shiftings that have ever accompanied our growth never found Seth Bullock at a loss; he was always ready to

"Turn a keen, untroubled face
Home to the instant need of things."

Throughout his well-rounded and picturesque career he coped with the varied problems that confronted him in that unostentatious and unruffled way so peculiarly his own, with which he faced the final and elemental fact of his recall from service.

ENDNOTES

CHAPTER I

[1] Fifteen years later when I was in Medora with Captain Seth Bullock, Muley was still alive and enjoying a life of ease in Joe Ferris's pastures.

CHAPTER II

[1] Shenzi really means bushman, but it is applied, generally in a derogatory sense, by the Swahilis to all the wild natives, or "blanket Indians."

CHAPTER V

[1] Since writing this we have heard from a friend who is learned in books. He tells us that he believes the letter to be an excellent facsimile pasted in the edition concerned.

SUGGESTED READING

AUCHINCLOSS, LOUIS. *Theodore Roosevelt*. New York: Henry Holt and Company, Inc., 2002.

BUELL, LAWRENCE. *The Environmental Imagination: Thoreau Nature Writing and the Formation of American Culture*. Cambridge, MA: Belknap Press, 1995.

BULL, BARTLE. *Safari: A Chronicle of Adventure*. New York: Viking, 1988.

CARTMELL, MATT. *A View to a Death in the Morning: Hunting and Nature through History*. Cambridge, MA: Harvard University Press, 1993.

COUPE, LAURENCE. *The Green Studies Reader: From Romanticism to Ecocriticism*. New York: Routledge, 2000.

GLOTFELTY, CHERYLL, AND HAROLD FROMM, EDS. *The EcoCriticism Reader: Landmarks in Literary Ecology*. Athens, GA: University of Georgia Press, 1996.

GRANT, GEORGE E. *Carry a Big Stick: The Uncommon Heroism of Theodore Roosevelt*. Nashville, TN: Cumberland House, 1996.

HALPERN, DANIEL, AND DAN FRANK, EDS. *The Nature Reader*. Hopewell, NJ: Ecco Press, 1996.

HOAGE, R. J., AND WILLIAM DEISS, EDS. *New Worlds, New Animals*. Baltimore, MD: Johns Hopkins University Press, 1996.

MCCULLOUGH, DAVID. Mornings on Horseback. New York: Simon & Schuster, 1982.

MORRIS, EDMUND. *Rise of Theodore Roosevelt*. New York: Random House, 2001.

NASH, RODERICK. *Wilderness and the American Mind.* New Haven: Yale University Press, 1982.

RENEHAM, EDWARD. *The Lion's Pride: Theodore Roosevelt and His Family in Peace and War.* New York: Oxford University Press, 1998.

ROOSEVELT, THEODORE. *The Man in the Arena: Selected Writings of Theodore Roosevelt.* New York: St. Martin's Press, 2003.

---. *African Game Trails.* New York: Charles Scribner's Sons, 1909.

---. *Autobiography of Theodore Roosevelt.* Cambridge, MA: Da Capo Press, 1985.

---. *Hunting Trips of a Ranchman and The Wilderness Hunter.* New York: Random House, 1996.

---. *Outdoor Pastimes of an American Hunter.* Harrisburg, PA: Stackpole Books, 1990.

---. *Ranch Life and the Hunting Trail.* Lincoln, NE: University of Nebraska Press, 1983.

---. *The Strenuous Life.* Bedford, MA: Applewood Books, 1991.

---. *Through the Brazilian Wilderness.* New York: Charles Scribner's Sons, 1914.

---. *Wilderness Writings.* Layton, UT: Gibbs Smith Books, 1986.

ROOSEVELT, THEODORE, AND JOHN GABRIEL HUNT, ED. *Essential Theodore Roosevelt.* New York: Gramercy, 1994.

THAYER, WILLIAM ROSCOE. *Theodore Roosevelt.* New York: Barnes & Noble World Digital Library, 2003.